ANGER MANAGEMENT

# KEEP YOUR COOL

*Secrets to Staying Calm and Collected in Difficult, Challenging, and Triggering Situations*

Luke Blake

from the Publisher. All additional right reserved.

The information in the following pages is broadly considered to be a truthful and accurate account of facts and as such any inattention, use or misuse of the information in question by the reader will render any resulting actions solely under their purview. There are no scenarios in which the publisher or the original author of this work can be in any fashion deemed liable for any hardship or damages that may befall them after undertaking information described herein.

Additionally, the information in the following pages is intended only for informational purposes and should thus be thought of as universal. As befitting its nature, it is presented without assurance regarding its prolonged validity or interim quality. Trademarks that are mentioned are done without written consent and can in no way be considered an endorsement from the trademark holder.

# Table of Contents

# PART I

# Chapter 1: Knowing Anger

Anger is a strong feeling. We all despise anger. Yet, none of us is without anger. It is a strong feeling of hostility or displeasure. Like happiness and sorrow, anger is also an emotional state. The state of anger can vary in intensity and expression. Anger could be expressed as mild irritation to a fit of rage or intense fury.

Most people believe anger to be a part of a person's personality. This is an incorrect approach towards anger, and as long as this approach is followed, managing anger would always be incredibly difficult.

You must understand that anger cannot be a part of the character of a person and expressed without reason. However, most of the time, the expression of anger is unreasonable, disproportionate, and undesirable.

*Benjamin Franklin once rightly said, 'Anger is never without a reason, but seldom with a good one.*

A person who is generally angry from everyone would also have reasons like disappointment, resentment, fear, and other such emotions inside, and the anger just works as a façade to hide a cocktail of such emotions.

Anger as an emotion can be broadly classified into two categories:

1. **Anger as a Primary Emotion:** This is the feeling of anger, irritation, or annoyance originating as a direct consequence of an action or event. This is a response that would originate inside you without a thought. It is

instinctive, unprocessed undiluted, and usually shortlived. If there isn't an escalation event, this anger will dissipate on its own as it is also inconsequential.

> *Example:* Someone driving rashly in front of you or jumping lanes without reason.

2. **Ange as a Secondary Emotion:** Anger as a secondary emotion can be dangerous as it is escalating in nature. Anger comes as a veil to hide other vulnerabilities, and hence it needs to be stronger and effective. Anger as a secondary emotion can be termed as a reaction to other emotions. Those emotions are stronger, more relevant, and forceful, but they remain hidden underground. The structure is similar to an iceberg where the anger is the visible tip that is sharp but may not be very significant in appearance, whereas the underlying emotions or the base of the iceberg can be enormous. Fear, frustration, hurt, rejection, and several other primary emotions can be hiding behind anger.

Secondary emotion can be more dangerous as it can completely overtake your rational thought process. It can get shunted off from the primary emotions and begin working on its own misdirecting you completely.

> *Example:* Road rage is a good example of secondary emotion. You begin an argument due to the frustration of being cut-off by another driver, but it soon gets escalated. Very soon, it doesn't remain about being cut off or not following the traffic rules. Feeling frustrated at being stuck in traffic is another example of anger as a secondary emotion. You feel angry as a

result of your frustration of not being able to go reach somewhere on time.

## Understanding Anger

You must understand that anger is a very common emotion. Every person on this earth feels anger. Irrespective of the person's beliefs or faith. However, some people can manage their anger well as they have mastered the art of understanding the cause and its effects. Whereas others are unable to manage their anger well and fall into the vicious trap of actions and reactions.

If you want to learn to manage your anger well, you must know the following things clearly:

1. **Anger** is also an **EMOTION**: Most people are never able to have any control over their anger as they are ashamed of recognizing it. Most of the time, they are simply trying to hide it under the covers. The key to managing your anger issues is to identify and accept anger like other emotions such as love, happiness, and sorrow.

2. **Everyone** Gets **Angry**: This is without exception. No matter who you are talking but you can be sure that the person in question feels anger for sure. It is a common and basic emotion. The only difference is that some people can understand the underlying cause of their anger and deal with the root issues, and others keep fiddling with the effects of the anger. The people who can get to the root cause will be able to deal with the issues more effectively, and hence a more dramatic display of anger wouldn't remain necessary.

3. **Anger** Has **Many Aspects**: What most people don't realize is that anger doesn't necessarily have to be linear. It can have several aspects, and hence there is no need to brush it under the carpet. When we do that, we are trying to get rid of things without understanding them. In this way, the problem doesn't get solved. It stays in its place.

4. **Anger** Can Be **Expressed Differently**: It is common for people to believe that anger can only be expressed explosively. This is besides the fact that most of us express anger in several different ways every day. The day you recognize them and learn to use them in your life, half of the problem would get solved on its own.

Anger is a very strong feeling, and it feeds on our state of mind. The more vulnerable we feel, the stronger the fire of anger would grow, irrespective of our position to express it at that moment or not.

You must understand that there is no way to eliminate anger from the root. The people who talk to acceptance, forget about limits. Anger as an emotion is always inside us. However, it can be both constructive as well as destructive, depending on your control over the djinn called anger. If you understand anger clearly and manage the way you allow it to come out, you'll be doing a great deal of good for yourself as well as for the society.

Management of anger through correct means is not only possible but very much practical. By ignoring anger management issues, you can be straining your relationships with the people around you and also with yourself. It can be constricting, suffocating, and humiliating to deal with your anger silently and dangerous if you let it loose. Anger management techniques can help you in letting it come out in a controlled and calm manner.

# Chapter 2:

# The Physiology and Psychology of Anger

Anger is a major event for the body. When you feel angry and agitated, it is not only your mind that's planning and plotting rapidly but also your body that's readying itself for a fight or flight response that might be needed according to your actions.

Therefore, broadly there are two parts of anger:

## The Physiological Impact of Anger

For the body, the angered state rings an alarm bell and activates the sympathetic nervous system. The muscles in the body start tightening up, and it can be termed as a part of the preparation to bear any physical attack.

Anger is also a part of our defense mechanism, and hence the blood pressure in the body rises along with the heart rate. All this is just to enhance the body's ability to react and attack. This mechanism has been designed to enhance our survival rate against a stronger opinion.

You could term the panic attacks as the flight response as that response is generally received when the opponent is undefeatable at that moment. However, anger response is generally fit for situations where you size up to your opponent, or you see a chance of victory. In such circumstances, your sympathetic system increases your heart rate and blood pressure. The hypothalamic nerve cells are also active, and they send messages to the kidneys to work up the adrenal glands.

They release large quantities of hormones like cortisol (the stress hormone) the adrenaline, and noradrenaline.

You need to note that the cortisol hormone helps in maintaining the level of blood pressure. Too much cortisol in the bloodstream can even cause high blood pressure levels.

In a crisis, these physical changes help your body in generating more force to defend itself or in launching an offensive. For that part, it can be considered a good thing, and it helped our ancestors. However, persistently high cortisol levels can cause serious bodily harm. First, it will lead to unhealthy blood pressure levels. High blood pressure can cause brain hemorrhages, strokes, and heart disease.

Anger as a part of nature can be destructive as it will cause serious physical as well as mental health issues. Victims of anger management issues are more likely to have stress-related disorders and problems.

## The Psychology of Anger

Anger is a very powerful emotion and can be very destructive at times. Anger can make you feel hard, crushed, and humiliated if you are not in a position to react immediately. On the other hand, anger-triggering thoughts, along with feelings of pain, threat, and sense of superiority, can also motivate a person to take aggressive action.

Psychologically, anger does offer a temporary boost of self-esteem and righteousness. Anger is generally a defense mechanism to avoid feeling vulnerable. Most of the time, people do not want to deal with their problems such as low self-esteem, helplessness, and vulnerabilities, and they use anger as a mask to hide these weaknesses.

However, the fact is that anger only masks these weaknesses and doesn't solve them or take them away. It can lead to several social and health problems that we have discussed.

Depression, social anxieties, irrational fears, social avoidance, fears, and complete isolation are some of the common mental issues that many people face due to anger issues.

# Chapter 3:

# Why Anger Management Is So Important

Anger is a malignant force and highly infectious. Your anger will not only eat you from within but also inflame your surrounding. A person with a short temperament and volcanic nature is always a burden for others. Even within the family, a safe distance is maintained from such people as an escape is not an option.

Anger may be a short term reaction to any problem or situation but it has a far-reaching impact emotionally, mentally, physically, spiritually, and biologically. We have discussed in detail the biological and psychological impact of anger on our bodies. Let us look at the ways it affects our bodies mentally, emotionally, and spiritually.

## Impact of Anger on Mentality

The most powerful and also the most dangerous thing about anger is that it shuts the logical brain and switches on the survival mode. This means when a person is angry, 'flight or fight' are the only two options in the mind of the victim and there is no process going on for resolving the issue. The mind is just thinking about temporary solutions. Now, this may or may not help the victim in avoiding the problem at hand momentarily, but it would certainly keep the mind occupied for long. Sometimes it passes without notice if the person is not feeling angry very often as the surge of anger would rise and then settle without leaving a long-lasting impact on the mind. However, if a person develops ager issues and starts experiencing the surge of anger with regularity, the mind would remain trapped in planning and plotting about others. The mind would remain riddled with negativity. This can make the mind toxic and highly insecure. This is one of the biggest reasons why anger management is so important.

## Impact of Anger on Emotions

One thing that we must never forget that anger is also an emotion, albeit a rather powerful one. When a person fails to manage anger and starts having frequent anger outbursts, it can give way to emotions that may hinder a peaceful life. Problems like increased anxiety, depression, insomnia, and the absence of mental peace are some of the signs that may emerge. Stability and certainty are conducive for emotional health but they get challenged when a person is struggling with frequent anger outbursts. Effective anger management is very important for emotional health.

## Impact of Anger on Spirituality

For many, spirituality is not even a subject of consideration. They believe that it is a topic fit for discussion only by the people approaching the end of the road. But, do you know,

- If you are having frequent episodes of anger or hopelessness then you might be suffering from spiritual distress
- Anger leading to anxiety and depression can also be a sign of spiritual distress
- You might also experience trouble sleeping peacefully

Spirituality is not just a subject of discussion at the end of life. We all have a spirit and a conscious. When we are angry, we do things that are not according to our consciousness. This can start hurting us knowingly or unknowingly.

Mark Twain once said, 'Anger is an acid that can do more harm to the vessel in which it is stored than to anything on which it is poured'. This must always be remembered by all who have anger issues of any sort.

Anger management is a must for such people so that they can find mental, emotional, and spiritual peace along with physical and psychological peace.

However, it is a fact that despite all the good advice some people might not pay attention to anger management. It happens with everything in life. People are repeatedly advised to quit smoking but they are unable to do so. They know alcoholism and drugs are deadly but they are unable to come clean. Anyone can overlook or pretend to unsee, but it is important to understand that the problem doesn't go away just because you aren't paying attention to it. The problem is inching closer to its target and getting stronger. The same is the case with anger management.

You can choose to ignore it but that doesn't mean the problem would become less gargantuan. The longer you ignore the anger issues, the deeper it would get imbibed into your nature and harder it would become for you to overcome the problem.

Dangers of Ignoring Anger Management

Ignoring anger management would increase the risk of health issues like heart diseases, strokes, poor immune system, anxiety, depression, and sleeping issues. Your lungs can get affected and it has a very big impact on your overall longevity.

Anger can make a person emotionally weak and volatile. It increases emotional insecurities and your ability to trust others goes down considerably. Anger increases the stress response in its victims and this means that your emotions can escalate easily and even on petty issues.

The University of Washington School of Nursing conducted a study on anger issues in husbands and wives. It found the poor anger management was a major cause of depressive symptoms and health issues in partners. The study found that while it caused women to experience depressive symptoms, it made men experience a large number of health issues.

An Ohio State University also found that people with poor anger management also have poor healing from wounds.

There are numerous studies to prove that anger issues are not just outbursts experienced due to some provocations but they are a symptom that something is wrong inside us and that needs to be managed.

If you or anyone you know is experiencing anger issues, then they must be addressed immediately as they can be the stepping stone for bigger problems in the future.

# Chapter 4:

# Correct Assessment of Your Anger Issues

The generalization or oversimplification of any problem is the first step towards making it unresolvable. We simply state that anger is bad. This is a general statement. This is not to say that any anger is good but then you'd have to devise a mechanism to stop it completely. There is no such mechanism possible for a natural emotion like anger and that is the core of the problem.

The statement 'Anger is Bad' is correct. However, there is no way you can cut it from its root because it is not an action but an emotion. It is coming from inside. A fact that usually gets ignored is that anger at every level is not even visible. Therefore, the correct way to deal with anger is to assess it correctly and then devise ways to deal with it in a correct measure.

All anger is not the same. If the anger is low, you might feel some emotions passing over you and it'd be gone. It doesn't have any long term effect. If the anger is mild, you are just causing harm to yourself. It can make you feel agitated, humiliated, and bad but it isn't expressed and whatever damage occurs stays inside you. However, when it breaches these levels, it can be harmful not only for you but also for the people around it. It is toxic, inflammatory, and exploding. For a better understanding, we can divide anger on a scale of 10.

**Scale 1:** At this stage, you simply feel irritated by a few things but you are easily able to ignore them. This usually happens when you are sitting with known or unknown people and listening to the things, ideas, and opinions you don't agree with.

**Scale 2:** You feel highly irritated and anxious but even at this stage you are in a position to think rationally and hence there is no demonstration of anger. This usually happens when you are getting badgered by the constant questioning of young kids or their childish behavior.

**Scale 3:** This is the stage where you feel irritated to the extent that you start responding sarcastically. You feel agitated but you can still think rationally and hence even at this stage any kind of altercation can be easily avoided. We usually demonstrate this behavior with our friends, family members, and colleagues. It is easily noticeable but not offensive.

**Scale 4:** This is the exasperation stage. At this stage, you may feel like shouting at the top of your voice and show your irritation and annoyance but you still keep it inside you. This is a laborious process and you may have to sugar coat your voice to hide your annoyance. However, even at this stage, your thought process is clear and in complete control. You can judge correctly.

**Scale 5:** This is the stage where your anger is visible on your face and in your behavior. Most people are still able to control an outburst of anger. The begin giving the silent treatment or hard looks but remain restrained to these. Their thought process starts getting muddled with angry thoughts but they are still able to control an outburst.

**Scale 6:** This is the stage of 'flight'. Your anger starts taking control of your mental dexterity. You are not able to push the angry thoughts from your mind and you are constantly thinking of ways to avoid that confrontation as you fear the negative outcome. Clarity of thought becomes questionable at this stage.

**Scale 7:** This is the stage where you start feeling cornered and the 'fight' response starts to kick in. The biggest problem at this stage is the mind getting hooked on to that angry thought and blocking any other idea. You start feeling tensed and the sense of 'right or wrong' and 'good or bad' starts getting fainter.

**Scale 8:** At this stage, retaliation becomes a clear plan of action. You want to say or do things that set the scores straight. Your thought process is completely obscured at this level.

**Scale 9:** At this stage, your angry emotions completely take over your rational thinking brain. Your words and actions are driven by your emotions. You are retaliatory and reactionary. You want to make others have a taste of their own medicine.

**Scale 10:** As you can imagine, this is the stage where there are no holds barred. You are thinking completely from your emotions and surviving this moment becomes your priority. This is the explosive stage.

Based on this scale, we can divide people into 4 broad categories:
This is a basic division that can help you understand the extent of the problem you'd need to deal with. The categories are self-explanatory from their names.

1. **Emotionally Stable:** If you are a person whose anger remains within the second scale, you are an emotionally stable person who has complete control over the mind and decisions. You have a positive outlook and you can take things in the right direction.

2. **Light Anger Issues:** People generally staying between 2-3 fall in this bracket. However, they know that their anger easily jumps to 5-6. These are the people who have had anger outbursts of level 9 or 10 a few times in their lives and they clearly understand the demerits.

3. **Volatile Anger Issues:** These are the people who are struggling with their anger. They clearly understand that their anger is usually on a scale of 8-9. They are completely unable to control their rage and it has become their nature. Even little things around them can cause them to explode. Such people can make the environment around them toxic. They can feel the discomfort people feel around them and some even start taking sadistic pleasure in it. Such people may or may not be physically abusive but would take pleasure in verbal abuse. These people need immediate professional help for anger management issues as they are not only causing harm to others but they are also becoming toxic for themselves.

4. **Volcanic Anger Issues:** These are the people who don't look angry or grumpy all the time but they can explode without a moment's notice. They are highly explosive in their behavior and may become physically or verbally abusive even on unexpected things. They become highly unpredictable and they can cause a lot of harm to themselves and also to others.

# Chapter 5: Understanding Simple Ways to Manage Anger

It is unhealthy to be angry. Yet, it is a fact that anger is an emotion and we all feel angry in varying degrees. The important thing is to keep this emotion under control. There can be external and internal events that may agitate you or make you feel angry. You cannot have complete control over such events. The important thing is to learn to control your reaction over such events. This is called anger management.

It is very much possible to manage your anger in most circumstances. If you are a person with volatile or volcanic anger issues then you'd also need professional help as your anger issues can take you on a dangerous path and they can be difficult to manage due to years of negligence. However, in others, the anger management process isn't very difficult, it simply requires a lot of practice and discipline. When the rage starts to develop in a person, the first thing that gets distorted is the clear thought process. Your mind gets completely focused on the event and the kind of turmoil it is causing in your mind. This will only lead to further escalation. The way out is to take your mind away from that raging thought and if possible think about the implications and the big picture.

The most important thing is the management of anger as and when it starts to develop. No matter your level of anger issues, if you can manage the ebbing anger in the initial stages, it would be far easier for you to avoid further complications or escalation. The initial management is crucial.

Although you might think that initial management is also the most difficult as very few people can avoid angry outbursts, this is far from being true. Most people are unable to avoid their anger outbursts because they have either never tried anger management properly or they lack practice.

In this chapter, we will learn some of the ways to manage anger better.

## Blowing Off the Steam Mentally

**Deep Breathing:** Deep breathing for many people may not sound to be such an effective tool but what they don't realize is the during the crucial moments when the rage is building inside you, deep breathing is the best and the most effective tool you'll have. People usually misunderstand the process of deep breathing and the purpose it has.

Deep breathing is an exercise to drive the mind away from the thought fueling your rage and focusing it on calming the body and the mind. You must remember that when you are feeling angry it is just not your mind but also your body at work.

For deep breathing, you neither need any equipment nor any preparation. You can do it while sitting in a room full of numerous people and none of them may take notice.

When you feel yourself getting agitated or sense the rage building inside you:

If you are standing try sitting down if possible
If there is no place to sit, please take some support
If you are sitting, please keep your back straight
If possible, close your eyes

If closing your eyes is not possible

Focus your attention at any point in your front

It can be any point, doesn't need to be any specific thing or marking


Now just try to normalize your breathing

We don't realize, but when we are angry

Our breathing rate increases

Just calm your breathing

There is no need to control your breathing

Just bring your focus on the way you are breathing

Notice if you are breathing fast or slow

With your awareness fixed on your breathing

Just try to notice your breath

Observe your breath

Keep breathing normally


Breathe in

Breathe out


Breathe in

Breathe out


Breathe in

Breathe out


Breathe in

Breathe out


Breathe in

Breathe out

Now observe, is your breathing calm now?
Are you still breathing rapidly?

Breathe in
Breathe out

Breathe in
Breathe out

Breathe in
Breathe out

Now, it is time for deep breathing
It is soothing and calming
You'll inhale through your nose
Very slowly
There should be no rush
You need to inhale as much air as possible
Keep breathing in as long as you can
When you feel full
Hold your breath
Keep holding it for a few seconds
Then exhale even slower than you inhaled
Do not rush your breath
Just push out all the air through your mouth

Begin inhaling through your nose

Keep drawing in air steadily

Keep your awareness fixed on the breath

Feel the sensation air makes at your nostrils

Keep sucking in air deeply

There is no rush

Keep your awareness fixed on your breath

Your mind may wander

You may have thoughts

There is no need to worry

There is no need to focus on them

Just keep your awareness glued to your inhalation


When you are full

Stop

You need to hold this breath a little longer

You might feel the pressure building inside you

There is no need to worry

This pressure is good

This pressure is healthy


When you feel unable to hold the breath anymore

Release it through your mouth

Very slowly and calmly

There is no need to rush

Just breath out all the air inside you

Let all the anger, anguish, and pain anguish get out with the breath

Push out all the anger from your gut


Relax!

Repeat the process several times until you start feeling calm and relaxed

Deep breathing is the most effective exercise in anger management that can help you manage even the most aggressive thoughts easily.

**Peaceful Mental Imagery**: Another effective way to manage your anger is to meditate using peaceful mental imagery. Most people misunderstand meditation as an activity that requires a lot of preparation and planning. They link it directly to spiritual pursuits. However, meditation is an amazing way to calm the mind. Although as opposed to deep breathing, you'd need to sit down for meditation, this is the only preparation you'd need.

Peaceful mental imagery requires you to close your eyes and focus on a happy, joyful, or pleasant thought that's very close to your heart. Deep breathing would help you a lot in focusing your mind on that pleasant thought but the very imagery in your mind would help in calming the aggressive thoughts in your mind.

This is an amazing way to blow the steam building inside you thinking about something that's not going to be pleasant for you or someone else. The easiest and fastest way to do this is to record something pleasant and calming in your voice in your smartphone or any other recording device and play it whenever you feel the need.

Peaceful mental imageries are very helpful in calming the mind and diverting it toward non-toxic actions.

**Loving Kindness Meditation**: This is a meditation exercise that you can carry out every morning. Loving-kindness meditation is very helpful in all kinds of anger issues. It is helpful for people who have mind anger issues as it helps them in staying positive. The people who have serious anger issues can also benefit from loving-kindness meditation as it motivates them to stay kind and forgiving throughout the day.

Please sit in a comfortable posture.

Keep your hands in your lap with palms facing upwards

Keep your spine erect

Please keep your neck straight

Do not use a neck rest

Now, please close your eyes

It is a simple exercise into kindness and forgiveness
It will fill you with love
You will feel kindness
You will feel gratitude
You will feel peace

It helps in healing wounds
It helps in recovery
It clears the heart of contempt

With your eyes close, remember the people you meet daily

Think of all the faces you see

The familiar faces

The unfamiliar faces

Some faces you remember

Some faces you don't

Some people are kind to you

Some are helpful

Some are recognizable

Some are inconsequential

But, all of them play some role in your life

It is important to remember them

It is important to think of them with gratitude


Breathe in

Breathe Out


Breathe in

Breathe Out


Breathe in

Breathe Out


Now, think of a person who has been very good to you

A person in your present

Or, a person in your past

A friend, a teacher, a parent, sibling, or any other family member

Any person whom you hold in high regard

Think of the love and affection showered by that person

Think of the feelings that come to your mind when you think of that person

Feel that love all over again

Feel that affection

Doesn't it feel good?

Feel the gratitude that arises in your heart


Now say aloud

I feel blessed

I feel loved

I feel nurtured

I feel the affection

I feel calm

I feel the gratitude


Now say aloud

May I keep feeling blessed forever

May I keep feeling loved forever

May I keep feeling nurtured forever

May I keep feeling the affection forever

May I keep Feeling Calm forever

May I keep feeling the gratitude forever


Now return the feeling for that person

May you keep feeling blessed forever

May you keep feeling loved forever

May you keep feeling nurtured forever

May you keep feeling the affection forever

May you keep Feeling Calm forever

May you keep feeling the gratitude forever

Now think of a person who might have helped you recently

A person who might have served you in some way but you don't know that person well

It can be a clerk in an office

A person driving the cab you took

A waiter who might have served you recently

It can be any person of that sort


Now think of that person

Think of the smile that person had

Think of the service that person gave you that you still remember that person

That person helped you or served you


Form a picture of that person at the back of your mind

Now say aloud


Thank you for your service

Thank you for your kindness

Thank you for your help

Thank you for being nice to me



May you feel blessed

May you feel calm

May you feel loved

May you feel nurtured

May you feel the affection

May you feel the gratitude

May you prosper

May you get happiness and joy

May you achieve all you want


Repeat this a few times


Now, think of a person you do not like

A person who may have been rude to you

A person who spoils your day

A person you may encounter even today

A person you don't like


There is no reason to hold a grudge

There is no reason to hate

There is no reason to be unhappy

It is easy to forgive

It is easy to forget the bad things in the past


Just say aloud,

I forgive you

May you also forgive me

May you feel blessed

May you feel loved

May you be happy

May you also prosper

May your life be filled with joy and prosperity

May you get all you wish for


May you feel my love

May you feel my gratitude

May you feel lots of joy in your life

May you stay healthy


Repeat these lines a few times


Now send out your love to everyone in the world

May all feel loved

May all be blessed

May all be happy

May all beings prosper

May all achieve their goals


Repeat these lines a few times


Keep breathing normally

Breathe in

Breathe out


Breathe in

Breathe out

Breathe in

Breathe out


You can open your eyes when you are ready.



# Blowing Off the Steam Physically


Sometimes the anger is very high and you start feeling highly agitated. These are the times when some people find it very hard to focus. At such times, it is better to give a physical release to anger. However, the physical release must come in the right way and under the right conditions. It must not be released in front of others and you must also ensure that no harm comes to you or others in any manner.

**Pillow Punching:** This is an easy and safe way to release your anger physically. If you are feeling highly agitated and you are unable to control your anger, you can punch your pillow to give your anger a physical release. You must do this only in seclusion and never on other things as it can even cause injury.

**Shouting It Out:** Shouting out is also a good way to blow out some steam. You can find someplace where no one can hear you or sit in the car with the windows closed and shout out the anger building inside you. This is much better than shouting at someone that can create a nasty scene. It can be very helpful in stressful situations as most of the negative emotions and energies get a proper release.

**Power Punching:** This is similar to pillow punching with the only difference being the replacement of a punching bag in place of a pillow. Power punching helps you in giving a powerful release to all your anger and it makes you feel relaxed. People generally feel much calmer after they have done some power punching.

# Chapter 6:

# Mindfulness and Anger Management

The Way to Seek Happiness, Inculcate Compassion, Gain Control of Emotions, and Channelize Anger Positively

For the uninitiated, mindfulness can be a difficult thing to understand. It is the practice of being fully present at the moment. This might sound so easy and simple, yet it has become so difficult to practice these days.

'Living in the Moment' is just not the motto of mindfulness but the whole and only principle.

Contemplation of the past and the worries of the future are the biggest causes of all kinds of stress in the world. The more you worry about them, the more worried, stressed, helpless, desperate, and agitated you'll feel. Not only this, worrying about the past and future also takes your focus away from the present where your life currently is. The simple principle of mindfulness helps you only on focusing on your present and letting the past and future be. The most difficult task in mindfulness is the art of letting go, and it will be the only challenge you'll face.

Mindfulness is the practice of keeping the mind calm and relaxed. When the mind is without the fear of the future and the agony of the past, it will react to things in the present normally. It is the practice of living every moment with joy and complete attention, and within this lies the answer to your anger. When your complete focus is on living every moment in the present, and you are rationalizing everything, you stop reacting to things instinctively, and the whole problem of anger lies there.

## Mindfulness Is the Practice of Being Aware

These are the times complicating even the simplest of things in life. Mindfulness is not a concept that should cause any kind of confusion. It is the simple art of being aware.

You need to be aware of every thought you have, every action you take, every decision you make, and you stop doing things in an auto-operated mode.

Mindfulness is the art of experiencing everything as a novel and complete experience. Even if you are drinking water, the experience should be immersive. You must feel the taste of water, the way it feels as it quenches your thirst, and the gratitude for the satiation it brings. Being aware of the whole experience is the art of mindfulness.

The only thing you need to be mindfulness is the simple art of paying attention. Now in this age of the internet, where the attention span of the millennials is just 12 seconds and the attention span of young ones in Gen Z is a paltry 8 seconds. Not only this, even within this fickle span of 8 seconds, but the Gen Z is also toggling between several windows. In such a scenario, it is very usual to sacrifice experiences and rely on automated information and reflexes, and that is the basis of the whole problem.

Mindfulness can help you in getting over this problem by encouraging you and giving you the right conditions to pay more attention to experiences and less value to memories and perceptions. Mindfulness teaches you the science of living in reality and staying away from perceived threats and memories. It helps you in living a real life.

For most people, this might sound a very difficult task to perform, and they are not to be blamed for that. Our lives have become so reliant of spoon-fed information and prejudices that even the thought of sensing everything paying attention to detail starts seeming like a tough task.

However, the beauty of mindfulness practice lies in the fact that it gives you the time to learn to enjoy these experiences. You can be practicing the first part of the process, and still, you'll be able to enjoy the process completely.

Four Important Principles in Mindfulness

**Non-judgmental attitude:** Judgmental attitude is among the most important reasons for increasing anger in society. We are quick to judge and label things as good or bad, right or wrong, or useful or useless. Such judgments come without a complete, fair, or thorough assessment of the object or person. This segmentation creates divides and stereotypes. We all are victims of such divisions and want a break for ourselves. Such divisions lead to anger, unrest, and inequalities. We all want freedom from such unfair divisions; however, when it comes to us, we don't mind following the stereotypes in our minds. Mindfulness helps in breaking such norms to allow you to a life where you don't judge others or get judged by them. Things don't get classified as good or bad. In mindfulness, every experience is just an experience. There is no need to record or memorize that moment for future needs.

**Acceptance of Every Experience:** Another big reason for the anger inside is our reluctance to accept fears, phobias, worries, inhibitions, weaknesses, guilts, indulgences, greeds, and other such things. We always try to remain free of every negative experience and then live in their fear for the rest of our lives. Mindfulness helps you in accepting every experience in life without any prejudice or fear. It helps you in experiencing and accepting the totality of every experience, thought, and feeling without taking into consideration the fact that they might be good, bad, or neutral.

**Readiness to Sense:** Another major roadblock in the path of anger management is our stubbornness to stick to the given patterns. We are not ready to feel anything new. We are unable to classify any new experience because we are simply looking for the non-existent set parameters. Mindfulness helps you in learning the art to approach everything with an openness to sense it in its entirety.

**Being Aware or Moving with Consciousness:** Consciousness or awareness are highly misused words these days. People simply keep using them generically even when they don't mean anything related to them. The words are very clear in themselves. Awareness or the state of being aware simply means having complete knowledge of the things happening around you. We live with the misconception that we are aware, yet most of us can't tell the pleasure of breathing or taking a deep breath inside. This is a basic act that we perform 24X7. Yet, very few people may have felt the sensation air makes as it enters the nostrils. This is a reason very few people think before they begin to react to anger. For managing anger effectively, the most important thing to learn is to become aware of the emotions in your mind. It is an act of being conscious of every thought crossing your mind or consciously, only allowing selective thoughts to proceed.

This is the way mindfulness can help you in managing anger effectively.

# Chapter 7

# 8-Week Anger Alleviation Plan

It is time to put your full understanding of anger and mindfulness into action. We understand that anger doesn't come from outside. It is an emotion that's inside us and comes out as a reaction. For every reaction, there needs to be a thought. Every thought originates in the mind. If you are mindful and you pay attention to every thought and reaction you give, managing anger would become very easy for you.

In this chapter, we will practice becoming mindful in our practice in 8-weeks. You must keep in mind that being mindful is a lifelong practice. The Buddhist masters following the Zen tradition of meditation practice mindfulness in every act they perform, and yet they can't be certain that they have achieved the desired perfection. Therefore, keeping the art of mindfulness in practice and making it a way of life is the best way to manage your anger through mindfulness.

**Week 1**

Ditching the Autopilot

As we have discussed at length till now, we all are living our lives on autopilot with no active control over our choices, desires, feelings, emotions, reactions, and experiences. This week, you must stop paying attention to what you know and pay attention to what you can discover and learn.

Simple acts like drinking water or breathing deep can be eye-opening experiences if you perform them with complete awareness. As an experiment, you should start performing deep breathing and chanting a positive affirmation.

This week, your complete focus must remain on doing everything with complete inclusiveness in the task. You must pay attention to every activity. If you are walking, you must be completely immersed in the act.

## Week 2

### Learning to Sense and Feel to Become Aware

Sensing is the second part of becoming aware. A big problem with the current age is that we are devoid of experiences. The world is full of critics, bloggers, vloggers, and reviewers who tell us about their experience of the things we want to enjoy. They enjoy those things and give us their views, which later on become our views, opinions, and experiences about those things. This is irrespective of the thought that we may have never seen those things or met those reviewers.

The biggest disadvantage of these things is that we are devoided of our own experience. If we read a negative google review about a food joint, not only our opinion changes, we might even not like the food irrespective of the taste it has to offer. It isn't the food but the rating that got rated by our mind, and it got precedence.

In the second week of mindfulness, you'll learn the art of feeling everything and experiencing every taste without judgment. This week, you must learn to feel everything through your senses.

If you are eating something, then you must identify that taste though your senses. The flavors it has and the way it tastes.

**Week 3**

Meditation and Exercise

In the third week, you must begin practicing meditation and exercises. Simple meditations and exercises will help you in not only becoming aware of the sensations outside, but they'll also help you in understanding your mind and thought process.

Meditation helps you in exploring your mind and your thought process.

In the beginning, you just need to sit in a cross-legged posture and focus on your thoughts. Try to look at the thoughts forming in your mind. Don't try to push any thought aside or intervene. Simply observe the process through which thoughts originate in your mind.

This is a very crucial step in the process of anger management as it helps you understand the basic process of thought processes. The better you'll know your thoughts and the way they form, the easier it'd get for you to manage your thoughts and emotions, and they'll lose power on you.

Practicing simple Yoga steps or other breathing exercises will be great this week. You must practice deep breathing asanas for several minutes a day as they help you in peering deep inside your mind. The deeper you focus on your breath, the easier it would become for you to stabilize your thoughts.

**Week 4**

Learning to Recognize Negative Thoughts and Mindful Walking

Once you have learned to peer into your mind and the thought process, you must identify the pattern of your negative thought process. In this week, you must learn to label your thoughts correctly and the way a thought begins and matures.

Understanding of negative thought patterns is very important in anger management as they play a key role in exciting and provoking you.

You should observe the thoughts very carefully and then follow their progression. There is no need for you to interrupt them or change their course. Even at this point, your objective should be to understand the way a simple thought turns into a colony of negative thoughts.

You should also begin expanding your area of attention, and mindful walking can be a very good step in this direction. Pacing up and down the room is an activity that most people carry out when they are lost in their thoughts. However, this is very different.

In mindful walking, you need to keep your complete attention on your walking. The way you raise your steps. The way it feels under the palm of your feet. The weight you feel on your legs. All your thoughts exclusively need to be about walking and the experience you are having.

This process helps you in understanding the way you can eliminate thoughts even when you are working.

**Week 5**

## Allowing Things to Be- Without Reacting Impulsively

This week, you'll learn to accept and acknowledge things without reacting to them. Avoidance of negative thoughts and escapism must be eliminated.

You must learn to accept every fact that comes in front of you as just a fact. You must not attach any significance to the thoughts or the facts. It is our habit of attaching significance that leads to problems. We attach a feeling and then make it significant enough to evoke an emotion that eventually gets expressed as anger.

Throughout the week, you will simply acknowledge the facts that come and then allow them to pass without judging them or attaching unwanted significance to them.

## Week 6

## Every Thought Is Just a Thought

This week is also an extension of the previous week, with the exception being that you'll follow the thought in your mind without attaching any significance to it.

This is the week to learn that every thought is just a thought. It is your mind that makes it scary or fun. A piece of news that might be heartbreaking for you may not mean anything for someone else. Its significance lies in the fact that you gave that news importance and emotion.

If you learn to label every thought just as a thought, managing anger would become very simple for you.

You must think of every negative thing that scared you until now and let it pass through your mind. You must allow it to pass through your mind in your complete awareness so that it loses its ability to scare you forever.

At this stage, your aversion to certain thoughts and ideas must come to an end.

## Week 7

### Learn to Be Kind to Yourself and Others

This is the week where you must learn to be kind to yourself and others. Practice Loving-Kindness Meditation in the morning and before going to bed at night. Learn to appreciate yourself and others at every step of life. Even if the task is not very big, learn to appreciate the effort and the things that have been done.

The more appreciative you become of yourself and others, the more difficult it would become for you to cultivate anger in your mind.

Practice this throughout the week.

## Week 8

### Becoming Mindful in Your Routine

This is the week of practicing your mindfulness routine with complete exposure. You don't have to be selective, and neither you have to be perfect. Cultivation of Mindfulness is a lifelong process, and it'd take a much longer practice than the short duration of a few weeks.

However, every journey starts with the first step, and you can consider these 8 weeks as your stepping stones into the amazing world of anger management through mindfulness.

# PART II

# Chapter 1: Back to the Basics

When most people think of mindfulness, they envision monks or yogis, sitting cross legged for hours with closed eyes and poised fingers overlooking the Himalayas. Although mindfulness is present in the lives of monks and yogis, what most people don't know is how easy it is to incorporate mindfulness into our everyday lives. As a matter of fact, a mindful state is the most natural and restful state for human beings—a state in which we were all living and moving in as children. If you think back to your childhood, you will likely remember that your concept of time and perception of reality was much different. Most children are very in touch with their emotions, letting them come and go naturally. If a child falls down in one moment and skins their knee, the child will likely begin to cry. However, if a few moments later they are being offered ice cream, their tears will dry, and they will continue on with their day. Mindfulness is the reason children are so in tune with the details of life that adults seem to miss. It is also the reason they are more likely to screech with joy, run around excitedly in enjoyable environments, wake up easily in the morning, and take the time they need to calm down from anger or sadness until the next happy moment arises. Children spend very little time thinking about things beyond the present moment. Even if they have something to look forward to, they are still likely to become invested in the moment at hand, whether that is playing, enjoying time with their parents, or eating a meal. So, what happens as people grow older that brings us away from this natural state of mindfulness?

There are a number of factors that pull people out of the present moment. From the time a child begins elementary school, they are presented with a schedule for the day, which remains relatively the same. Children are expected to remain within the structures presented to them, and the idea of forward-thinking and preparing for the next hour's activity becomes introduced. As they grow, children will likely have more expectations placed upon them, whether those expectations are academic, extracurricular, or within the home. Of course, it is necessary for children to learn how to be responsible and dedicate the time they need to the important things in life. However, as they become further exposed to the constant rush and future-oriented thinking of their parents and teachers, they come to see time as something that no longer belongs to them to fully inhabit.

Furthermore, as people approach teenage and young adulthood, they will begin to face challenges that most children are either shielded from or otherwise unaware of. People become flooded with the pressure to perform well and always be doing more today than yesterday. Although the expectations of cultures and societies vary, we can be sure that people are overwhelmed with the pressure to meet those expectations in order to be considered successful and valid. Once one bar is crossed, another one is waiting, and there is no time to slack. Additionally, the older people become, the more likely they are to be subject to long-lasting pain in their lives. This can come in the form of relationships ending, failing to accomplish something, being mistreated by other people, losing and grieving loved ones, or coming to terms with painful childhood events that did not make sense at the time. Teenagers become increasingly subject to mental health issues as they advance into adulthood, having to face all of the hard realities of the world and still come out on top. People may also be subject to trauma as a result of illness, accident, or abuse. All of these factors are enough to work against people and pull them out of the present moment, either because it is too painful to be there, or because they are simply too distracted.

Human beings experience over 60,000 thoughts per day, but the vast majority are dedicated either to planning for the future or worrying about the past. Becoming overly concerned about the future or steeping in the pains or regrets of the past can increase levels of stress in the body, which makes people more anxious and prone to physical health problems.

The mind naturally wanders, and it is impossible to keep thoughts from coming. Mindfulness is not a tool to eradicate such thoughts, as is the common misconception. Rather, it is a tool through which to acknowledge the thoughts the mind creates, bring attention to them, and allow them to move through. This ultimately brings people into what is happening here and now and gives them more control over their minds and how they orient themselves in their environments.

Because mindfulness is a skill that all human beings are equipped with at our core, it is something that can be re-learned. Just as we exercise our bodies to strengthen our muscles, so we must work to strengthen our brain through mindfulness. The way this strengthening happens is through being aware of thoughts as they arise, then breathing back into the present moment. The more practice is given to returning to the present moment, the stronger the mind will become in remaining in the present more often. Just as the body physically strengthens and becomes healthier over time with exercise, mindfulness exercises can physically change the structure of the brain to make it healthier. Mindfulness activates the positive components of the hippocampus, which is the part of the brain responsible for good things like creativity, joy, and the ability to process emotions. This, in turn, decreases stress levels, depressive tendencies, addictive behaviors, and the fight or flight instinct by shrinking the part of the brain responsible for negative things (the amygdala). Overall, increased mindfulness is the key to a longer, healthier, more creative, and more joyful life.

## Chapter 2: Unlocking Your True Purpose Through Mindfulness

Re-centering Yourself

Everyone has days where everything seems to be spinning out of control, and there seems to be no way to manage the chaos. The days where you wake up late, run late to work, spill coffee on your shirt, get cut off on the road, get yelled at by your boss, spend the entire day at work in a confused frenzy, only to come home and bicker with your partner. Since the beginning of time, the human mind has been conditioned to release stress hormones and illicit the fight or flight instinct for the purpose of protection and survival. In the past, this primal instinct was very useful for escaping threats. As times have changed, the threats have become less severe, but the brain's response has remained largely the same. Now, these fight or flight reactions are likely to be triggered by everyday scenarios, such as those previously detailed. The hormone-induced responses that occur when we're stressed out are quick to send us spiraling into emotionally dramatic, and far less peaceful dimensions.

The good news is, mindfulness can be used as a tool for re-centering and gaining control over your anxiety and emotional reactions when you start to feel yourself spiral. Although there is no way to avoid stress and drama in daily life, mindfulness can serve as a shield of calm presence to protect your well-being. If you are preparing to enter a situation that you anticipate could be stressful, like a high-stakes day at work, a scary doctor's appointment, or a difficult conversation with a loved one, it can be incredibly helpful to bring yourself down to a more calm and balanced state in preparation for the stress you are about to deal with. You may find yourself with a racing heart, sweating palms, an unclear head, and the feeling of "butterflies in your stomach." Another area where it is common to feel these physical effects of anxiety is when encountering dramatic situations. Drama can arise tense moments with other people, as well as within the theoretical situations people create for themselves when worrying about what they cannot control (for example, the perception other people have of them, or events that may or may not occur in the future). Giving attention to what is happening in your mind and body and allowing yourself to breathe into the moment can be a total lifesaver in moments of drama or stress. Two to three minutes of deep breathing in your car before going to work, or taking a few deep breaths before reacting in a tense moment, can make a drastic difference in your sense of balance and your ability to deal with stress without launching into fight or flight.

## Giving Your Emotions Space

The goal of mindfulness is not to eliminate emotions, but rather, to gain control over the impact they have on how we orient ourselves in the world. It is vital to honor our emotions and give them space to exist and teach us, without letting them seize control. Mindfulness is an excellent tool for giving our emotions space in this way. When an emotion arises, mindfulness gives us a chance to observe that emotion without judgment. In this calm space, we can ask our emotions, "What are you trying to teach me?" We can more clearly discern why we are experiencing a certain emotion, and become in touch with the deeper needs that may have caused that emotion to arise. Just as a child may cry when they need to be nourished our held, we may find ourselves growing angry or agitated when we need support, touch, or self-care. Similarly, we may find ourselves feeling stressed or anxious in scenarios that are subconsciously triggering moments from the past. In these cases, our stress and anxiety are begging us to become in touch with our past self, reminding ourselves that we are safe, and the traumatic moments from the past are over. Once our emotions have been given a non-judgmental space to exist, they can smoothly and peacefully move through the body and be released. This frees us to move from moment to moment like children do, without being constrained by unresolved emotions. Additionally, giving this space to our emotions in mindfulness helps to temper our reactions, which can prevent us from acting out in extreme ways and potentially doing or saying something we regret.

## Making Clear Decisions

With the human mind constantly being muddled with thoughts, it can be hard to see things clearly. Sometimes our minds are cluttered by the expectations flying at us from every different direction, or perhaps by our fears of what will happen if things don't go to plan. When it comes to making decisions, we are often faced with numerous options, and it can be difficult to navigate through the chaos in our minds to come to a well thought out resolution. In a distracted, anxious, or removed state, our minds are like a pond on a rainy day—rippling to a point where there is no more clarity. Mindfulness is the calming of the waters, which brings us to a place where we can more clearly think of all possible outcomes of a decision and check in with what we truly need before moving into the next moment.

## Keeping Yourself Safe

Although fight or flight instincts originally developed as a way to keep humans safe, in many modern-day scenarios, they do quite the opposite. Let's go back to the example from the beginning of the chapter about the chain of events in a typical chaotic day. If you wake up late in the morning and rush to make your coffee, not paying attention to what you are doing, you run the risk of haphazardly screwing the lid on your to-go cup, then sloshing boiling hot coffee over the edge of the cup and onto yourself as you bolt out the door. Although such a scenario could simply result in a stained shirt, the inattentiveness could have a more drastic effect, such as burning yourself or someone else. Driving to work in a state of panic over running late causes you to be more likely to break the rules of the road— driving too fast, making dangerous decisions when changing lanes, taking turns too fast, running yellow lights just before they turn red, etc. Additionally, the panicked state can lead to anger with yourself or others on the road, which can further impair judgment and put you at greater risk of an accident. Attempting to have a conversation with your boss if you are in fight or flight mode could result in being overly emotional and saying or doing something extreme which could place you at odds within your workplace, potentially even costing your position. Going throughout your day in a frenzy causes you to be less aware of what is going on around you, which can lead to further threats to safety like leaving a burner on, forgetting to eat or drink enough water, or neglecting those in your care (such as pets or children) as a result of your own inner distractions. Finally, as stress from the day carries into the home at the end of the day, it can pose a major threat to relationships. The more stressed out and less clear thinking you are, the more likely you are to say or do something threatening to your partner, to put yourself in an aggressive and volatile situation, and to make brash decisions that have the potential to haunt your future.

Improving Relationships

Just as we must give ourselves space to learn, grow, and process our experiences, we must give that space to those around us as well. When a partner or friend is acting in a way we don't enjoy, mindfulness can allow us to take a step back and look at the situation from a position of empathy. We can allow ourselves to hold space for whatever that person may be going through individually and express our support while also maintaining boundaries and staying in control of what we can. Everyone is deserving of space to be listened to, understood, and supported for who they are. However, it is incredibly difficult to give that space to anyone if it has not been cleared within oneself.

When we operate out of a mindless state, there is hardly any space to meet our own needs and process our own experience, much less to provide that to other people. This can lead us to be closed off to the ones we love, push them away, or act out in anger, selfishness, or aggression. If we have not given space to what is going on within us, we cannot offer full empathy to others. Only 20% of the population is recorded to practice true empathy, which can be linked to the rarity of true mindfulness among adults. Mindfulness allows us to be more present to our own needs in order to hold adequate space for the needs of others as well.

Attention and mutual respect are core elements of every functional relationship. Practicing mindfulness can improve relationships with all the people in our lives by preparing us for every engagement and calming our minds enough to be fully present in the moments we share with others. Mindfulness clears the space for us to listen intentionally to other people and pay more attention to what kind of people they are and what kind of support they need. It allows us to love other people better by increasing our awareness of how they feel most loved. By being present in the moment at hand, as opposed to trapped in the past or future, you are more likely to remember to pick up the phone and give your grandmother a call, to be fully engaged when interacting with your child, or to remember the kind of kombucha your significant other likes best from the store. Not only does mindfulness allow for more meaningful conversations and joyful memories, but it also increases the functionality of our relationships overall so that both ourselves and those we love are feeling fully respected, listened to, and encouraged.

## Fostering True Joy

We often hear the term "childlike joy" to describe moments of pure bliss, enthusiasm, and full satisfaction. As people grow into adults, such moments tend to be few and far between, with many remembering the most joyful moments to have been those that occurred in childhood. The expectations of daily life become too much, and most people find themselves trapped in a cycle of constant anticipation. People spend so much time thinking about where they would rather be (on vacation, in bed, enjoying the weekend) that the days melt into each other without us realizing all the moments of our lives we are missing. The biggest societal misconception is that true happiness lies in what we do not yet have. We are flooded with lies such as "Once I can buy this new TV, then I'll be happy," or, "Once I have a partner, then I'll be happy," or, "I'll be happy once I can say I've been to five different countries." Mindfulness abolishes these lies by proving to us that the capacity for true joy lies not in the future but in the here and now. Wherever you are right now, whatever you have, and whichever stage of life you're in, mindfulness reminds you that *this* is your chance to experience beauty and satisfaction like never before. Take time to look at the flowers you did not notice growing in front of your neighbor's house, the complexity of coffee's flavor as it slides down your throat, the way your loved one's eyes crinkle when they smile, the laughter of a child, every intricate flavor of dinner, or the unique people wandering up and down the streets you drive every day to work. It is here that joy resides; all you have to do is be present enough to recognize it.

# Chapter 3: Moving Mindfully in Daily Life

Coming to the Present Moment: Daily Guided Mindfulness Meditation With Journaling (Week 1)

*Cultivating Mindfulness*

This meditation should be done in a space where you feel fully comfortable, safe, and relaxed. Perhaps it is in a corner of your bedroom, in a garden, by your favorite lake, or even in your car. Make sure you can fully relax and avoid distractions. Some people meditate best with instrumental music or nature sounds in the background, while others prefer silence. Feel free to try multiple methods and see which is most soothing to you (this can vary depending on the day). You may do this meditation sitting in a chair, on a mat, or lying flat on your back with your palms up to the sky. You will need to give yourself 5-20 minutes of time to practice, depending on your skill level and current state. If you like, you can set a timer.

Start by coming into the moment with a few deep breaths. Settle into your body and take note of any sensations you feel. If you feel pain, tingling, warmth, or tightness in any part of your body, focus your breath into that space. Imagine any tension unfurling into openness. Notice as your thoughts arise. Take notice of them, then allow them to pass as you come back to the breath. If it is helpful, you can try a breathing pattern in order to culminate focus. To do the 4-4-4 breathing pattern, breathe in for 4 counts, hold for 4 counts, and breathe out for 4 counts. To do the 5-5-7 breathing pattern, breath in for 5 counts, hold for 5 counts, release for 7 counts. Sometimes it helps to imagine breathing in the things you wish to see more of in your daily life (creativity, love, patience, openness) and exhale the negative things (fear, negativity, sadness, stress). Allow yourself to spend a few moments in a more active state of breathing in, releasing, and paying attention to your body.

With practice, you may enter a state where your thoughts slow and you become fully grounded in the present moment. In this state, you are no longer bombarded with thoughts, nor distracted by elements of your environment. It becomes easier to return to the breath. All restlessness and tension in the body seem to melt away, and the mind reaches a flowing, liquified state. There may be days when you cannot enter into this state, and you remain restless throughout the course of the meditation. If this happens, allow it to be that way, observing every thought that arises, then letting it go.

After the time is up, begin to arrive in the moment by moving your body slightly—wiggling your fingers and toes, tensing and releasing your muscles, etc. Next, you're your eyes. Notice how bright and clear the world looks to mindful eyes. Notice the calm, transcendent feeling in your body, and continue to move with it as you go about your day.

**Mindfulness Meditation Journal Prompt (Week 1):**

*What did you feel in your body before beginning? What do you feel now?*

*Which thoughts continued to arise in your consciousness? Could these thoughts have been trying to teach you something or speak to a deeper need you may have?*

*How does the world look after opening your eyes? What do you notice?*

*Come back after going about your day for several hours. Did you bring mindfulness with you into the world? If so, how?*

Coming to the Present Moment: Daily Guided Mindfulness Meditation With Journaling (Week 2)

*Taking Mindfulness Into the World*

This meditation will be done with your eyes open in moments if your daily life. This is not a specific meditation you have to set aside time for, but rather a state you come into. Notice where your attention goes in a given moment. If your attention is drawn to a particular sight, like the nearest tree or a view from the top of a mountain, allow yourself to see it fully. Repeatedly tell yourself, "see, see, see." Breathe as you allow your eyes to truly become totally focused and take in the image fully, allowing it to become a part of your awareness.

If your attention is drawn to an auditory experience, such as the sound of cars on a city street, a rushing body of water, or an internal monologue, give full attention to that thing. Soak in that auditory experience, breathing slowly and telling yourself, "hear, hear, hear."

You may also be drawn to a particular physical or emotional experience within the body. This experience may be positive, like a pleasant bodily sensation or a feeling of joy. It may also be negative, like physical pain, or feelings of anger or feel. Either way, allow yourself to become fully present with what is there, breathing into the experience and seeing what it has to teach you. Breathe into that bodily experience, telling yourself, "feel, feel, feel."

Throughout the day, you'll find that your attention is pulled in various directions. Mindfulness is the choice to tune in to whichever place you're going in a given moment and give full attention to that experience for whatever it is.

**Mindfulness Meditation Journal Prompt (Week 2):**

*How difficult was it to bring mindfulness into your daily life in this way? Where did you face the most challenges?*

*Did your attention tend towards certain experiences (visual, auditory, bodily) more than others?*

*Describe a specific moment where you brought mindfulness to your experience and felt truly present. What did you observe?*

Coming to the Present Moment: Daily Guided Mindfulness Meditation With Journaling (Week 3)

*Mindfulness at Work (or School)*

The first part of this meditation should happen in a place outside of work, where you feel safe, calm, and separated from the issues you may face in the workplace. Start by identifying your biggest struggles at work. The journal portion will give you a space to write them down. Do you struggle with productivity? Boredom? Stress? Conflict resolution? Work relationships? Once you have identified your most significant area(s) of struggle, close your eyes and visualize what that unpleasant experience looks like. Perhaps it looks like you, rushing around mindlessly like a bee in a hive, stressed out and too overbooked to step away and breathe because there are more calls to make, more e-mails to send, more things to do. Or, perhaps it is the co-worker, professor, or boss that makes your stomach drop whenever you think about having to interact with them. Perhaps you feel unfulfilled at work and find yourself constantly checking the clock, thinking about the moment you get to leave. Maybe you have so many things to do and no idea where to start, so you waste a lot of time on mindless tasks. Whatever your struggles at work are, use your time and space away from work to safely visualize the situation. Breathe into the mental circumstance.

As you breathe, begin to envision what this experience would look like if it went the way you want it to. Perhaps it looks like the mental clarity that allows you to know exactly what needs to get done and how to make the best possible use of your time. It could be a greater sense of calm and courage when talking with your difficult boss or co-worker and having your message be well-received on their end. It may also be a deeper sense of satisfaction and enjoyment in the work you're doing, providing you the ability to step back and feel a sense of joy with where you're at, without constantly thinking about the next thing. Reframe the moment in your mind until you've created a mental space that feels good. Let yourself sit there, breathing, soaking it in for several minutes.

Once you go into the workplace (or school), you can bring this meditation into your life by going back to the peaceful mental image you've created over and over again. When you begin to feel stressed, bored, anxious, or unproductive, return to the space where you do not feel those things. Bring that energy into your daily work life, and watch how it revolutionizes your experience.

## Mindfulness Meditation Journal Prompt (Week 3):

*What do you identify as your biggest challenge(s) at work or school?*

*How does it look when you reframe your struggles to create a positive mental image?*

*What do you observe about bringing this positive mental image into difficult situations in the workplace or at school?*

Mini Meditation Toolbox: 15 Quick and Easy Meditations to Integrate Mindfulness Into Your Daily Life

*One-Minute Mindfulness*

- Find a space where you can be alone, like on your bathroom break or in your car right before going into work, school, or home at the end of the day.

- Set a timer for one minute

- Close your eyes and focus exclusively on your breathing

- Take notice of the stresses, thoughts, and anxieties that arise, then let them go

- When you open your eyes, notice how you feel de-stressed, clear-minded, and prepared to go about your upcoming tasks and interactions with others

*5-Minute Body Scan*

- Set a timer for 5 minutes (if needed)

- Close your eyes and take several deep, cleansing breaths. You may use the 4-4-4 or 5-5-7 breathing patterns to deepen the breath

- Begin to bring attention to your body

- Take notice of any sensations that arise-- warmth, tingling, tension, etc.

- Bring your attention to the soles of the feet. Tighten your muscles by curling your toes, then release. What sensations do you feel?

- Continue moving up the body to your calves, hips, abdomen, chest, hands, arms, face, and neck. Observe any sensations that arise, and breathe into those sensations.
- Tighten and release the muscles in each of these areas, allowing any pent-up energy or resistance to be released
- Feel your body become grounded, relaxing completely into the floor, bed, or chair as you come into the present moment in your body and all tension melts away

*Mindful Bath/Shower (10-minute meditation)*

- As you begin your bath or shower, take a moment to breathe. Remove yourself from the stresses of the day and allow yourself to re-center
- Bring attention to each part of your body as you wash it
- Take notice of any sensations you feel as you move from the soles of your feet to the ends of your hair
- Breathe in the pleasant scent of the soaps and the warmth of the water. Allow yourself to feel clean, warm, and safe.
- As you wash each part of your body, thank it for what it does for you. Then, thank yourself for taking care of your body.

*Mindful Morning Routine (15-30 minutes)*

- Before getting out of bed, begin to stretch gently, letting thoughts come and go as your mind and body wake up. Do not rush yourself.

- Once you are ready to get out of bed, bring your attention to the space around you and the day ahead. Feel yourself become fully present in that space and prepared to move mindfully through your day

- Pay attention to every move you make, from putting on clothes, to washing your face, to setting the water on the stove to boil.

- Cultivate your awareness for the day ahead by moving slowly and calmly, one task at a time, becoming fully awake to the world

*Mindful Housekeeping*

- Allow yourself to become focused on the task at hand and only that task. Let every other thing you have to do or think about fade into the background.

- Bring your attention to the breath and the specific way your body moves as you complete a particular task or chore

- Give space to any thoughts or emotions that arise in your consciousness, allowing yourself to process them in a mindful state

*Mindful Sit-and-Drink (10-minute meditation)*

- Find a calm, quiet space where you can sit and observe the world around you (preferably outside or near a window looking outside)
- Pour a glass of your favorite tea, coffee, or cocktail to enjoy
- Eliminate all distractions. Draw your attention to the intricate flavors of the drink, and the pleasure of pulling something you enjoy into your body
- Take notice of the things happening around you. Find the things in the environment that bring you the most peace, and allow their presence with you to help you calm your mind. Become completely indulged in the moment.


*Mindful Scheduling (10-minute meditation)*

- Sit down with a pen and paper and center yourself with five deep breaths.
- Think about the days to come. Consider your priorities, remembering that every task is significant and an opportunity for increased mindfulness
- Ask yourself, "Am I giving myself adequate time to bring mindfulness and intentionality into each of these activities?"
- Take notice of any activities you feel you won't be able to be fully present for. Consider taking a thing or two off the list and saving them for a better time.
- Take notice of any feelings of stress, nervousness, or rush you feel in regards to your schedule. Breathe into those feelings.

- As you continue to write your schedule, allow yourself to feel empowered, in control, and prepared to be mindful of everything you are about to do

*Mindful Driving*

- Leave the house with plenty of time to be relaxed and focused. After entering the car, take a few moments to breathe and center yourself
- Once you start to drive, begin to take note of the things passing by. What do you see today that you did not see yesterday?
- Breathe in your visual surroundings, using them to center and remind yourself: "I am here. I am in this community. This is my life, and I am awake to it."

*Mindful Walking (10-20-minute meditation)*

- Choose an area where you can relax and bring attention to your surroundings. This can be in a park, in the city, on the beach, in your neighborhood, etc.
- Set out on your walk with no distractions
- Take notice of the things your eyes fall upon. If something specific catches your attention, allow yourself to pause and breathe it in.
- Pay attention to the sounds that surround you, giving yourself space to truly hear them

- Pay attention to the feeling of your feet on the pavement, the swing of your arms at your sides, and the rhythm of your breath

- Let your heart expand in curiosity and openness to whatever is ready to meet you in this space

- Allow yourself to become totally saturated with your surroundings, remembering that everything you see, hear, and feel is a part of you

*Mindful Cooking and Eating*

- As you enter the kitchen to prepare food, take a moment to center yourself in the moment with a few deep breaths

- Give every moment of the cooking process your full attention, from washing, to cutting, to cooking. Become fully immersed in the process (you can do this even with simple meals, like mindfully spreading peanut butter on bread)

- Breathe loving-kindness into the cooking process, remembering that the food you make will provide nourishment to yourself and others

- Once the food is ready, clear the eating space of distractions. Avoid multi-tasking

- Chew every bite of food 20-30 times, letting yourself be engulfed in the flavor and practicing gratitude for the nourishment

- Walk away from your meal feeling truly nourished and renewed

*Mindful Waiting*

- The next time you're trying to distract yourself at the doctor's office, the mechanic, or waiting for a friend or colleague to arrive, remind yourself that waiting is one of the most sacred times to engage in mindfulness

- Breathe into the moment, becoming aware of what surrounds you

- Bring awareness to your body. How are you feeling? Take note of any sensations

- Become aware of the thoughts that come once you stop numbing yourself with distractions. What things are running through your mind?

- Pay attention to the deeper thoughts you may have previously been ignoring. Ask yourself what you can learn about yourself and your life, or if there are any actions you need to take.


*Mindful Creativity (at least 5 minutes)*

- Set aside anywhere from five minutes to several hours of undivided time

- Engage in a creative project like art, writing, dancing, etc.

- Bring full presence to the creative project and try to eliminate all expectations. Allow the moment to carry you.

- Pay attention to how your mind and body react as the moment carries you. How do you feel?

- Examine what you create as a result of this free-flowing creativity

*Mindful Play*

- Dedicate time each week to doing something truly fun—something that makes you feel like a kid again (climbing a tree, swimming in the lake, drawing with chalk, baking cookies, having a game night, etc.)

- Eliminate all distractions and allow this to be a moment to step away from your everyday life and responsibilities

- Allow yourself to become lost in the childlike joy of play. Laugh loudly, let your body dance, be curious.

- Let the feeling of childlike joy saturate your body and carry this joy with you as you move back into your daily life.


*Mindful Movement* (10-30 minutes)

- Choose one of your favorite forms of movement (swimming, walking, dancing, going to the gym, etc.) and dedicate at least ten minutes to it

- As you begin to move, establish a deeper sense of body awareness. Pay attention to the feelings in your body as you begin to warm up and exercise

- Pay attention to the way your heart beats, your lungs heave, your face begins to sweat, and your body tingles with the sense of being alive

- Thank your body for all it does for you.

*Mindful Listening/Quality Time*

- Apply this meditation to any quality time you spend with another person, whether that is grabbing coffee or going for a walk with a loved one, interacting with co-workers, are conversing with the grocery store cashier

- Before interacting with others, bring attention to your levels of empathy. Set the intention to hold space for other people and the moments you share with them

- Eliminate distractions (like technology) and allow yourself to put everything else going on in your life on pause in order to be fully present

- One of the best ways to show love for people and to cultivate personal mindfulness is through mindful listening. Focus all of your attention on the other person and what they are saying. When you ask how their day is going, be present to hear the answer.

- Do not think of what your next move will be, what you will say, or where you will go. Simply be there, showing loving-kindness, holding space, and taking it all in.

Mini Meditation Toolbox: 10 Quick and Easy Meditations to Ease Stress, Depression, Addiction, Anxiety, Pain, Distraction, and Loss Using Mindfulness

*Journaling the Consciousness (10-minute meditation)*

- Sit down with a journal and a pen and set your timer for 10 minutes
- As thoughts, worries, or emotions arise, immediately write them down. Do not worry about structure, grammar, or content, just write.
- When the time is up, look over what you wrote
- Ask yourself which themes seem to reoccur. Where are you feeling stress in your life? What is occupying most of your mental space?
- Close your eyes and take a few moments to breathe and meditate on the thing(s) that need your attention the most
- Open your eyes. Notice how you feel lighter and in touch with your experience

*Distraction Cleanse: Clearing the Space in your Mind*

- *Find a quiet place and begin to breathe*
- Ask yourself: "What is distracting me from being present right now?"
- Give space to that distraction, whether it is an invasive thought, personal emotion, or someone else's emotion

- Say to yourself: "I am letting my distractions move through me as I ground myself in the present moment. Nothing is more important than right now."
- Breathe until you feel the distraction melt away into presence and mental clarity.

*Re-Writing the Moment: A Short Meditation to Ease Emotional Pain of the Past*

- Sit down with a journal and a pen and set your timer for 1 minute
- Take this 1 minute to write down any moment(s) of the past which have caused you a lot of pain
- After the minute is up, choose one of the painful moments, close your eyes, and begin to imagine the moment in a safe way. Be sure to keep breathing.
- When you open your eyes, take your pen and paper and re-imagine the painful moment. What do you wish had happened? How do you wish you could think about the moment now?
- After re-imagining the painful moment, remind yourself that this is a new moment. Everyone has painful memories, but you do not have to stay in spaces of the past, which are painful for you.
- Close your eyes, take a few more breaths, and say to yourself, "I release the pain of that moment of the past. This is a new moment, and I will move with it."

*Re-claiming your Inner Power: A Short Meditation to Face Addiction*

- Breathe into the moment, allowing yourself to think about the implications your addiction has on your life

- Without judgment, question your addiction. Ask yourself, "What has been left empty in me that I am trying to fill with this?" Listen for any emotions or past experiences of trauma, grief, or abandonment that arise. Allow them to be there.

- Say to yourself, "Now that I understand the root of my addiction, I can begin to be set free."

- With closed eyes, begin to breathe. With each breath, imagine your addiction's hold on you weakening and weakening until eventually, you have been released.

- Move forward into your life with the idea that your addiction's hold on you is loosening, day by day.

*Letter to the Lost: A Short Meditation to Address Grief and Loss*

- Sit down with a journal and a pen and take five deep breaths to bring you into the moment

- Allow someone you have lost to come to mind. This can be a relationship that has ended, someone who has died, etc.

- Close your eyes and breathe into the space this person has left empty within you. Allow yourself to experience any emotions that arise.

- When you open your eyes, take a few minutes to write what you wish you could have said to that person

- After you have finished your letter, close your eyes again. Tell your grief that it is okay for it to be there. With every breath, imagine yourself moving forward in your life, released from every regret you may have with someone you've lost

*In with The Positive, Out with the Negative: A Short Breathing Technique*

- Find a comfortable space and prepare to use the 5-5-7 breathing technique
- Breathe in for five counts and think of something positive you want to bring into this moment (kindness, peace, wisdom, etc.)
- Hold for five counts, allowing this positive thing to fill your body
- Exhale for seven counts, thinking of something negative you want to release from your body in this moment (stress, tension, selfishness, etc.)
- Begin again with a second emotion. Do this as many times as you like until you feel well-equipped with positive emotions and have released all negative ones

*Space to Breathe: A Short Meditation to Gain Control over your Anxiety*

- When you begin to feel anxious, step away, take a breath, and ground yourself in the moment by finding one thing you can see, one thing you can hear, and one thing you can feel. Focus deeply on each thing.

- Allow your anxiety space to exist. Remember, anxiety is the reaction your emotional brain has when it senses a threat. You can bring yourself back from catastrophe mode by using the rational brain to repeatedly remind yourself: "I am safe. I am in control. I am capable of being calm."

- Keep breathing and saying these rational-brained affirmations until you begin to feel your anxiety melt away

- Move into the next moment feeling calm, anxiety-free, and empowered

*Emotion Coding: A Short Meditation to Bring you in Touch with your Emotions*

- Find a quiet, comfortable place where you can easily connect with yourself

- Close your eyes and breathe deeply (you may use a breathing pattern if desired)

- Begin to travel inwards. Say to yourself, "I am ready to accept the emotions that are here."

- Wait patiently, focusing on the breath, and observing every emotion that rises to the surface.

- When an emotion arises, ask yourself a series of questions:

  1. "Is this emotion mine or someone else's?"
  2. "Does this emotion serve me or hold me back?"
  3. "What is this emotion trying to teach me?"
  4. "Should I release this emotion or put it into action?"

- When it comes to answering each question, listen to your intuition. The answers to each question are already within you. Do not question your natural answers.

- If you are being told to release an old or negative emotion, or an emotion that belongs to someone else, breathe and imagine it melting away with every exhale

- If you are being told to foster a positive emotion or a strong emotion that can create positive change in the world, sit with that, breathing, and being open to how that emotion can be useful.

*The "I Love…" Gratitude Meditation (2-minute meditation)*

- Find a private space, preferably one in front of a mirror

- Start a timer for 2 minutes

- For two minutes, speak out loud sentences of gratitude beginning with the words "I love…" ("I love my partner," "I love coffee," "I love my cat," "I love sunflowers," I love my mom," "I love to dance," "I love that I am healthy,").

- Say as many things as you can, one after the other. Do not think too much, simply let the things you love flow from your lips

- When the timer goes off, look in the mirror and say "And I love you," to yourself

- Feel the magic of gratitude transforming your life, your self-confidence, and your ability to be mindful

*The Mindful Manifestation: A Short Meditation to Manifest what you Want in Life*

- Sit down with a journal and pen

- Begin to cultivate mindfulness by bringing attention to your breath and any sensations in your body

- Ask yourself the question: "What do I want most in life?"

- As the answers start to come, open your eyes and begin to write your desires with the words "I manifest…" in front of them ("I manifest empathy." "I manifest peace of mind." "I manifest protection." "I manifest safety." "I manifest love." "I manifest awareness." "I manifest wisdom." "I manifest pure joy.")

- With each manifestation, close your eyes, and say it to yourself at least three times. Feel this manifestation become a part of your reality.

# PART III

# Chapter 1: What is CBT?

None of us have control over every aspect of our lives. Therefore, we all must play the hands we are dealt as we navigate through life. Unfortunately, many of the circumstances we have to deal with are unpleasant and can leave us with lasting scars that can start a domino effect of negative thoughts that seem to never end.

It is important to understand that our ability to control many of the elements in our lives is out of our hands; we can't even control the thoughts that seem to flow endlessly through our minds. Still, this does not mean that we are completely helpless. While much of these things happen against our will, there are many things we can do to change the situations we face. At the very least, we can control how we respond to the external events and factors we deal with from day to day. We have the ability to control our reactions to events, thoughts, and internal beliefs about what is happening to us.

This adjusted kind of thinking is at the heart of CBT. It is a research-based approach to a treatment that will address a wide variety of mood and anxiety disorders. A fundamental belief behind CBT is that after experiencing certain situations, certain thoughts are developed in the mind. These thoughts lead to a variety of different feelings (many unpleasant), which can trigger negative reactions. Since feelings are not that easy to change, the concentration of the therapy is on challenging the thoughts that trigger those feelings and once you can control your feelings, you will be able to control your actions. As you develop these new skills, you will be able to manage your life better, which by extension, will allow you to build up a more positive view of the world, and thus have an improved pattern of behavior.

So, rather than pouring out your past to a therapist, opening up painful wounds of the past, and examining every minute detail of them, you and your therapist will work together to discuss the problems you are facing today, set a series of goals, and then apply different strategies and exercises you can apply to help you achieve them.

## The Science Behind It

Unlike psychoanalysis, a common form of therapy developed by Sigmund Freud, where treatment is based on early life experiences and uncovering hidden memories that may have been buried, CBT takes an entirely different approach in healing the mind. In CBT, the problems are the foundation for the treatment.

In the early part of the 20th century when psychoanalysis was the accepted form of treatment, you would have spent an endless number of sessions talking about your past. The psychoanalyst would likely interrupt your dialogue with occasional questions about what you might think this image or that person meant, forcing you to think deeper about your reaction to certain events, people, and influences in your life. His goal would have been to get you to explore hidden messages stashed somewhere in your psyche.

At some point, the treatment would gradually take effect and your feelings would start to experience a change. This form of treatment, while effective, would often require a long-term commitment, which could take years to complete, if ever.

About the middle of the 20th century, we began to understand better how the brain worked. Initial research into the function of this organ started focusing on the more recent scientific discoveries relating to both animal behavior and then later in the field of metacognition.

As scientific research progressed over the last century, they have been able to develop a better understanding of learning, behavior, and cognition (our thoughts); it was a natural progression from Freud's form of therapy to what we use now. First, experimenters began to recognize that even animals could associate two separate events together. For example, an experimenter would ring a bell and then give food to a dog. After this action was repeated several times, the dog would automatically associate the bell with food. It was apparent that the dog understood that the sound of the bell meant food.

The next progression was the discovery that helped us understand how human behavior developed. Scientists wanted to understand what would make a person more likely to do one thing and less likely to do another. It was quickly understood that if you punish someone for an action (giving them an unpleasant result), then they would cease the action. The opposite was true with a reward system. If a reward was given, the individual would then be encouraged to continue the action.

This knowledge was quickly applied to mental health where they could now focus their attention on treating the behavior of a patient rather than rehashing all of its past experiences. The patients that are most benefited from this type of therapy are, in a sense, stuck in a certain pattern of behavior. The trigger for that behavior may have happened in his or her childhood or it may have happened in the past few months. The time of the trigger or the real nature of it is not as important as addressing the present state of affairs. The therapy, therefore, is focused on changing that behavior so that he can get out of his rut and start living his life again.

The next evolution of CBT was developed much later in the 60s and 70s. The focus then was on identifying what was really triggering that behavior. It was determined that it was the power of the thoughts and their effect on emotions, which in turn, was triggering the actions. Psychiatrists recognized that to understand how a person feels, they must first understand what a person was really thinking. If a person is struggling with anxiety, then chances are their thoughts were full of thoughts of danger or risk.

Up until that point, they had recognized the cause and effect scenario that was playing out in a person's mind. For example, someone who is afraid of elevators would see the elevator and automatically feel fear.

What they realized later was that there was one missing element that needed to be understood. It wasn't the elevator that was causing the fear in the person, but it was their mind's interpretation of what that elevator actually meant. This goes back to the original premise that what a person thinks is what dictates his emotions and his behavior.

However, we all know that what we think and believe is not always accurate. According to his book *Healing the Addicted Brain*, Dr. Harold Urschel explains that once you begin to analyze your thoughts, you will inevitably find inaccuracies in your reasoning. These inaccuracies tend to reappear over and over again in your mind until corrected. In other words, all of us have distorted thinking and need to be aware of them. In fact, just the simple act of recognizing and acknowledging them will automatically make it easier to change your thought process and help you to replace them with healthier thoughts.

So, if one can get inside the thought process and find the flaw, correcting certain behaviors could be addressed simply by correcting the wrong thoughts that were playing out in their mind at the time. This means that if a person was struggling with irrational thoughts, these could be replaced with more realistic beliefs through a process of challenging them and arming them with a new way of thinking. Analysts were no longer focused on finding the root cause of a problem and could now focus on changing the thoughts that trigger unwanted behaviors.

Through CBT, analysts could help their patients by giving them a set of skills that could be learned, practiced, and through a regular application on their own, could work independently to address their issues.

## How it Works

As you read these words, the whole process sounds relatively simple. At first glance, you might have even wondered why a person would need a therapist to figure this out, and you'd be right. But, for those who are stuck in that endless loop of unwanted behavior, it still remains a real challenge.

It is a huge step from Freudian therapy to CBT. A person has to first come to the understanding that three core elements of our human makeup are completely interconnected: our thoughts, feelings, and behaviors. It is literally impossible to change one without changing either of the other two.

This concept can be illustrated simply. If you are struggling with feelings of anxiety, it is usually because your mind is overwhelmed with thoughts of dangers that you want to avoid. However, if your thoughts of danger are distorted, then your reaction to those thoughts will be strange, out of the ordinary, and even extreme. It is only a short step from a fear of danger to trigger our fight-or-flight response, which will either cause us to avoid the situation altogether or to take an aggressive stance.

**The Basic Principles of CBT:** In order for CBT to be effective, there has to be a good relationship between the therapist and the client. At the very least, there must be a mutual respect for each other and it is extremely important for the therapist to get a good understanding of how the client sees things.

From this area of mutual respect, the foundation for treatment can be laid. After that, there are several other basic principles that must be followed:

- CBT is not an open-ended therapy session – it has a time limit. In most cases, the time with a therapist runs only 10-15 sessions. This puts a slight pressure on the client to not procrastinate in getting started with the specific steps the therapist will give him as homework. He is less likely to put it off until a more convenient time.

- CBT is based on more than a century of research studies. From the beginning, a therapist can give a pretty reasonable estimate as to how long a program can run given the client's unique mental state of mind, and how much of a benefit he can expect to achieve in that time period. As they work together through the sessions, it will be easy to see which parts of the program are working well and which ones are not and make adjustments accordingly.

- CBT always has a very specific objective for the client. It is not about looking at the past but is more about achieving a specific goal. You can't make progress if you don't have a direction to go in, and it won't take long before you will see evidence that the program is helping you to get to the behavior you want to display.

- CBT is a team effort. The therapist doesn't "fix" you. You work together to address and discuss out a certain issue. Each party in the team has something to contribute; the specialist understands just how CBT works, and you (the client) understand how you work. Bringing the two together, as a team, allows both to tailor a treatment that will address the specific needs of the client.

- CBT is well-organized. CBT sessions are not hours of aimless ramblings with a therapist. Instead, they have structured in such a way that the patient knows exactly what his objectives are and the steps they are going to take to get there. The first sessions are dedicated to creating a roadmap outlining every step in the treatment plan. Throughout the program, both the therapist and patient can check to see if they are still on course or if adjustments are needed.

- CBT is about the present. While CBT looks at past events in a patient's life, its primary focus is on what can be done today to fix the problem. It stresses the importance of finding ways to change thoughts and behaviors today so that there can be immediate relief.

- CBT involves action. Both the therapist and the patient are fully engaged in the process. Without a commitment from both parties, it won't be successful. From the very beginning, it requires both to be fully involved with each stage of the treatment.

- CBT focuses on skills. Patients go through each therapy session learning different skills they can continue to use once the session is over. These skills teach you how to identify the mind games you play with yourself, the self-sabotaging strategies you use, and teach you how to stop those bad habits in their tracks and choose healthier and more productive options.

- CBT stresses practice. You have 168 hours in a week and can count on only one hour of time with your therapist. So, in order to get the most out of each session, it is important that you practice each of the strategies learned in your session on your own. The more work is done in between sessions the faster the progress will be.

## Changes Thought Patterns and Belief Systems

Since Cognitive Behavioral Therapy is based on the evidence that our *perceptions* of the situations in our lives dictate how we feel emotionally, our perceptions of the world are, therefore, the direct result of what we think is really happening or will happen. These are the elements of our lives that need to be adjusted.

For example, an individual may find something in this book and think it is exactly what he is looking for. Because he **believes** it is beneficial for him, he then feels good and perhaps even relieved to have found the solution to his problem. However, another person may read the same information and feel entirely different. He may believe that it isn't the right solution for him or that following the exercises are beyond the scope of his ability. As a result, he will feel disappointed and maybe even discouraged at not finding the answer to his problem.

In theory, it is not the experience that causes people to feel the way they do, but it is their perception of the situation or their thoughts about the experience that needs to be modified. We all understand that when a person is under stress, their viewpoint of a situation is often extreme, inaccurate, and unrealistic, so if it is the perception of an experience that triggers negative habits, then this is the area that needs to be focused on.

With CBT, people are helped to identify those negative thoughts, give an honest and realistic appraisal of them, and then learn strategies to help them to readjust their distorted thinking. Once they are able to think more realistically, they will begin to see things differently and it will be easier for them to adjust their behaviors. The therapy works within a narrow focus of solving their immediate problems and making behavioral changes.

## Its Purpose – Who it Can Help

Of course, CBT is not a catch-all for all psychological disorders. It has proven to be most effective for the treatment of anxiety, depression, and other forms of mood disorders including obsessive-compulsive disorder, bipolar, and PTSD. While the National Institute for Health and Care Excellence (NICE) specifically recommends CBT for the treatment of anxiety and depression, there are many more mental health issues that it can be very effective with.

Because of its unique flexibility, the therapy can easily be adapted to a wide range of needs. There is a whole list of psychological issues that can be benefited by it including:

- ADD/ADHD
- Alcohol abuse
- Anger management
- Anxiety
- Bipolar disorder
- Borderline personality disorder
- Chronic fatigue syndrome
- Chronic pain
- Depression
- Drug abuse
- Eating disorders
- Facial tics
- Insomnia
- Obsessive-compulsive disorder
- Phobias
- Post-traumatic stress disorder
- Psychosis
- Relationship problems (individual or couple's therapy)
- Schizophrenia

In most cases, it can be a very effective form of treatment without the use of medication, but in extreme cases, where the symptoms a patient is experiencing are severe, a doctor may suggest the use of medications to make it easier to get into a mental state where patients can effectively apply the strategies suggested as they go through the program.

## How it Works on Anxiety and Depression

When dealing with anxiety disorders, one must first come to understand the true nature of anxiety. While unpleasant in many ways, a certain level of anxiety is necessary for life. Without it, we would find ourselves in an even worse predicament. Consider all the ways a healthy sense of anxiety can be of benefit.

Both anxiety and fear are natural forms of emotions. They serve as your body's personal alarm system and can occur as a warning sign that there may be some kind of risk or harm present. Fear, a heightened sense of anxiety, appears when a person is literally faced with a dangerous situation. Anxiety occurs when they "expect" that something unpleasant is about to happen.

A good example of this is taking a ride on a roller coaster. The feeling you get as the car is slowly pulled up that first big hill. You are in anticipation of what you know is about to happen as soon as you reach the top. Fear is the feeling you get when you are plummeting down the hill.

Both emotions are warnings and can trigger all sorts of bodily sensations. They tap into our flight-or-fight response so that we can quickly respond to those warnings, allowing us to flee, freeze, or fight. These instinctive emotions have been a part of us for as long as the human race has existed. It is a highly developed system that allows us to react quickly without having to put forth a lot of effort. They make it possible for us to have an automatic response.

The problem with these emotions is evident when they become overactive. It is natural for humans to have a very active imagination that allows our minds to create certain scenarios that we may encounter. For example, you may be anticipating how a certain job interview will play out. Your mind may conjure up something good or something very bad, both could result in anxiety even though there is no assurance that what you imagined will actually happen. This is evidence that our internal alarm system can be triggered even when there is no real threat to deal with.

The natural progression is that if our automatic thoughts are negative, we will respond accordingly. As a result, if we have conjured up images of a bad interview, our reactions could be so strong that we can take some very negative actions that could harm us in some way. For example, we might refuse to show up for the interview, we might choose to apply for a job that we find less challenging or risky, or we might become so flustered that we blow the interview altogether causing our worst fears to come true. These choices could actually have a very negative effect on our lives causing us even more harm in the future.

Anxiety and depressive disorders can appear in a variety of forms. Episodes may be occasional or they may be constant. If these automatic thoughts are not addressed, they will only become more sensitive starting a spiral effect that will send a person deeper and deeper into a level of anxiety that will be even more difficult to get out of.

CBT is most effective because it works to correct those automatic thoughts. Those spontaneous thoughts we all have that spring to mind without prompting. Automatic thoughts start before we are born and will continue unabated until we take our last breath. It is our brain's way of processing the millions of bits of information it is constantly receiving from our five senses: sight, sound, smell, taste, and touch. If the brain receives any input from these sources under a stressful situation, it can create unfounded assumptions about a given situation or possible outcome. These negative assumptions create an unhealthy internal dialog that could build up to a point that it prevents an individual from progressing when faced with similar circumstances. Unless this internal dialog is corrected, the resulting negative emotions or behavior could take control causing the person to be paralyzed to the point of inaction or to exercise complete avoidance.

So, how can you tell if you have normal anxiety or have a disorder? Mental health professionals often refer to the *Diagnostic and Statistical Manual of Mental Disorders (DSM-5)* for the guidelines for making a diagnosis. An anxiety disorder is diagnosed when:

- The anxiety one experiences are excessive: being afraid of snakes may be normal but being petrified of worms would be considered extreme.
- The anxiety is constant and can last for weeks or months at a time: there are different time frames for each type of disorder. For example, when panic disorder symptoms last for a month or more, it can be diagnosed as an anxiety disorder. However, for generalized anxiety disorder, the symptoms must be present for a minimum of six months.
- The anxiety itself causes more anxiety: when a person becomes really upset by the mere fact that they are experiencing anxiety.
- The anxiety interferes with a person's normal activities: when you can't walk outside of your home, go into a public place, or can't work on a job because of the heightened level of anxiety.

There are several different types of anxieties that could be considered an anxiety disorder. They are very different from each other, so before treatment can be started, one must understand exactly what type of disorder they have.

**Phobias:** Phobias are powerful and irrational fears of a particular object or situation. Common phobias could be a fear of anything from snakes to something that is part of the natural environment. Most common forms of phobias might be an extreme fear of storms, flying, elevators, spiders, and even people. In many cases, these start with a traumatic experience, but not always. Sometimes, the actual cause of a phobia is never discovered.

**Social Anxiety Disorder (SAD):** These are fears of social situations. In these types of cases, the fear is often confined to the fear of embarrassment. SAD is different from other phobias because it often involves the mind "guessing" about what is going to happen or what someone else might be thinking. With other phobias, we may know that the thing we're imagining can actually happen. We know about dog and snake bites; there is plenty evidence of the consequences of such events, but social phobias are more likely related to what one might be thinking rather than as a result of what they believe.

**Panic Disorders:** Panic disorders usually come about without warning. Many often mistake a panic attack for a disorder, but panic attacks that might be experienced are usually the symptom of the fear or phobia of a certain situation.

The attacks come on suddenly like a loud alarm going off in the body. The sympathetic nervous system instantly triggers a "fight-or-flight" response that is very physical. It releases a huge dose of adrenaline into the system to help prepare the body for danger. As a result, the person will experience:

- Rapid heartbeat
- Faster and deeper breathing
- Dizziness
- Profuse sweating
- Digestive problems
- Tense muscles

A person may experience some of these symptoms or all, but the concept here is that the symptoms are not just a little change but are quite extreme.

**Agoraphobia:** Interestingly enough, agoraphobia is not a very specific phobia but is the fear of being in places where you feel it would be bad to have a panic attack. This causes the person to avoid public areas such as movie theaters, shopping centers, public transportation, etc. If they go anywhere at all, it is usually in the company of another person they feel is safe and would be able to help them if something were to happen. In extreme cases, the patient is reluctant to leave the house at all and may squirrel away inside for years at a time.

**General Anxiety Disorder (GAD):** This disorder presents itself as a persistent and pervasive sense of worry. It is not the normal concerns of everyday life that most people have but is so intrusive that it interrupts sleep, keeps the individual from concentrating which leaves them to feel exhausted all the time. Unlike other anxiety disorders, GAD is also evidenced by anxiety and worries that are spread out over a number of different areas. It is not specific to a single type of fear, thus the name of General Anxiety Disorder. The individual's life is plagued by a never-ending worry about "what ifs" to the point that they can no longer function normally.

People who suffer from panic attacks, phobias, obsessive thoughts, and a never-ending stream of worries about everything will gain the most from CBT. This type of therapy, unlike medications, treats much more than just the symptoms that you may have. It can help to reveal the underlying causes of those incessant worries and fears. As a result, patients learn to relax and see each situation in a completely fresh and less intimidating way. They become better at coping and learn how to think through all of their problems.

There are many different types of anxiety disorders, so each session will be tailored to the specific problem of each patient. For example, for those who may be struggling with obsessive-compulsive disorder (OCD), their treatment will differ greatly from someone who is struggling with an anxiety attack.

The therapist will work with them to first identify the negative thought and then teach them through guided sessions on how to challenge those thoughts. For example:

Negative thought:       What if I have a panic attack on the subway? I'll pass out!

Distortion:       Believing that only the worst can happen.

Challenge:       Have you ever passed out on the subway before? It's unlikely that you will pass out on the subway.

Negative thought:       If I pass out, terrible things will happen.

Distortion:       Expectations clearly out of proportion with reality.

Challenge:       If I do pass out, it'll only be for a few seconds. That's not so bad.

Negative thought:       People will think I'm crazy.

Distortion:       Drawing conclusions you know nothing about.

Challenge:       People are more likely to show concern and help.

In the beginning, these thought challenges will be guided with the therapist, but in time, the patient will learn to do these themselves. For milder cases, an individual can work these out for themselves with the use of a CBT workbook. Negative thinking doesn't just happen all on its own but is an accumulation of a lifetime of negative influences. While it sounds simple here, it can be quite difficult to remold one's thinking into something that is more positive. Those suffering from anxiety and depression disorders will:

- Learn to identify anxiety and how it feels in the body
- Learn skills to help them to cope and relax to counteract the anxiety
- Learn to confront their fears (real or not)

Of all the psychological disorders you can find, anxiety is by far the most common.

- 18% of anxiety disorders are phobias
- 13% are social anxiety disorders
- 9% are general anxiety disorders
- 7% are panic disorders
- 4% are agoraphobia

## Depressive Disorders

Depressive disorders come in a different form. Many may start with some type of injury that renders them unable to function for a time. This triggers a train of losses or disappointments of many of the things the person may use to enjoy. The loss of these once fulfilling activities starts him on a downward spiral where he begins to believe that he doesn't deserve them or that he's done something that has triggered the loss.

A depressive disorder can make it difficult to function in any capacity. They may feel like everything they do is ten times harder than it used to be. It could feel like trying to pull themselves out of a quicksand and they may feel that they are so pathetic or worthless that it is not worth putting up the effort.

Most people only know depression as a feeling of sadness, but its symptoms can vary widely depending on the type of depression they are experiencing. It can present itself in many forms. In many cases, the patient has no idea that he or she is dealing with depression, because often, the symptoms do not present themselves as they would expect.

**Major Depressive Disorder:** Another term for someone who is "clinically depressed" is a major depressive disorder. This can be described as a person who feels low for the better part of the day. However, while this is a very common symptom, it is not necessary for them to feel an overwhelming sense of sadness to be considered depressed. It could be evident in their lack of interest in any activities, many of which they may have used to enjoy.

At the same time, they may sleep excessively, eat more than usual (whether they are hungry or not), or stop eating altogether. They feel exhausted and have a hard time concentrating on what they need to do or even making decisions.

While we all have a tendency to feel bad about ourselves at one time or another, those who are clinically depressed feel so bad about themselves that they believe they are completely worthless and are at a very high risk of suicidal tendencies, so they need to be watched carefully.

According to DSM-5, there are nine different symptoms of depression; five are needed to be observed in order to be diagnosed as clinically depressed. Because of this, the condition of depression may look very different from one person to the next.

**Persistent Depressive Disorder:** There are ebbs and flows of a major depressive disorder, where the individual may feel up and good at times but at other times, they may struggle to even get out of bed. With a persistent depressive disorder, however, the symptoms may seem to be more chronic. To be diagnosed with a persistent depressive disorder, they have to experience symptoms consistently for a minimum of two years before they are diagnosed. In addition, they need to display at least two more symptoms listed in the DSM-5.

With a PDD, the symptoms can be milder, but its negative effects can be extreme. While the symptoms may not appear to be as severe as an MDD, one can never assume that its effects are not as bad. At times, the symptoms can be even more destructive because of their chronic nature, as the individual never gets any sort of relief from the pervasive symptoms.

**Premenstrual Dysphoric Disorder:** This type of depression usually appears just before and for several days into a woman's menstrual period. It is important to understand that this is not the same thing as PMS (premenstrual syndrome). The condition is much more extreme with women displaying volatile mood swings and irritability. In addition to feeling anxiety, they can often show physical symptoms as well including breast tenderness and bloating. The symptoms should appear before or during most of her menstrual cycles for as much as a year before being accurately diagnosed.

Getting diagnosed with an anxiety or a mood disorder is not always easy. In fact, the process can be quite complex. Each form of depression has to have a number of different labels that identify exactly which type of depression the person may be dealing with and its nature. In addition to the main symptoms listed above, there may be seasonal depression, postpartum, a form of melancholy, single, and recurrent episodes. Whatever the case, there is a good chance that applying CBT techniques can help to manage all of these symptoms. One of the first things an individual needs to do is to get an official diagnosis. Once the diagnosis is completed, the next step is to sit down and work out how it is affecting you in order to determine the goals you want to work towards and a time frame in which to complete them in.

## How CBT Helps With Substance Abuse

While CBT is most often used for anxiety and depressive disorders, there are many more mental health issues that it can also help with. It has been highly effective in preventing the relapse of problem drinking and drug addictions. These are common behavioral patterns that can be readjusted by redirecting the thought processes that trigger the abuse of many substances.

A key element of CBT is teaching the patient to anticipate situations and give them practical strategies to help them to cope effectively when these conditions arise. These strategies could include things like analyzing consequences before a decision is made to use the substance, self-monitoring themselves so they can identify cravings at the onset, and avoid situations where they might be at a higher risk of using.

By learning to develop strategies that will help them to better deal with cravings and those situations where they will find themselves more vulnerable, they can reduce and eventually eliminate their use of these substances

With the treatment for substance abuse, the objective of CBT is to:

- Help the individual to identify those situations where they are more likely to use alcohol or drugs
- Help them to develop strategies to avoid such situations
- And to identify common problems and triggers, which could cause them to abuse substances

This is done through two major components: function analysis and skills training.

With functional analysis, the therapist and the individual works to identify certain thoughts, feelings, and environments that historically have led to substance abuse. From this, they are able to determine the level of risk the patient is likely to face, or under what situations could expose them to a potential relapse.

CBT also will give them special insight into what started them on the path to substance abuse in the first place. Then they will give them coping strategies, so they are equipped to handle similar situations in the future.

With skills training, the individual will learn better coping skills. They will work on unlearning those old habits that took them in the wrong direction and replacing them with healthier habits that will be of benefit to them. In other words, they will be educated about how to change their thinking so that they are better able to deal with the varying situations that will trigger more episodes in the future.

To date, more than 24 different trials have been conducted with substance abusers of all sorts including those who are addicted to alcohol, cocaine, marijuana, opiates, and tobacco. In each of these studies, CBT has proven to be one of the most effective forms of treatment in helping to restructure their recovery. However, it is not the catchall answer for everyone. Because each person is different in the nature of their problems, everyone will respond to this type of treatment in a different way. Still, the results speak for themselves and if you or someone you care about is struggling with some form of substance abuse, there is a good chance that they will learn something and gain some benefit from incorporating CBT into their lives.

# Chapter 2: How CBT Can Help With...

We live in unpredictable times and every one of us may be expected to address a number of issues at any given time. It can be a pretty stressful life for most of us. However, if someone is dealing with intrusive thoughts on top of the problems they face, it can become a complex maze that they may struggle desperately to get out of.

Dealing with any problem is not really the issue for these people. When a situation arises, the difficulty occurs with the manner in which he or she may address it. If their solution is based on distorted thinking, it can create a myriad of new problems in addition to creating a snowball effect. People who are plagued with unrealistic and intrusive thoughts are usually more reactionary rather than taking a proactive approach.

CBT's goal-oriented approach encourages a hands-on and more practical direction which teaches the patient that there is a means to an end. They do this by making a comparison between where the individual is at the start of the problem and then working out the best path to take to achieve the set goal. The ultimate goal is to change the thought pattern, which in turn, will change how they feel, and by extension, their behavior. In this way, CBT has been used to treat a wide variety of problems that range from sleep disorders to relationship issues.

On the surface, the logic of CBT is very simple: change one's negative thinking to positive thinking. However, this is not always easy. It requires that the person first learn to identify the negative thought processes they have. This requires them to take a hard look at themselves and give an honest appraisal of how they really think.

This may involve applying a little mindfulness and seeing their thoughts as a neutral person. When they see that their views are overly negative or overly positive. They will be compelled to learn to adopt a more balanced view of themselves, those around them, and their environment; viewing everything as a neutral person. This kind of adjustment takes time, as they may not fully realize just how far their thinking has strayed from the normal way of things.

Patients need to learn how to identify when their thoughts are triggering negative emotions and when to stop them before this happens. Then, they need to examine those thoughts honestly to determine if they are truly giving a fair and honest appraisal of the situation; how realistic they are and how damaging those thoughts are to them.

This helps them to avoid falling into thinking traps (negative ways of viewing things) so they don't fall into the problem situation in the first place. These mental traps could become major landmines that could quickly throw them into a world of trouble. These thinking traps are often negative words they would never say to others, but they say it to themselves.

Consider if you don't like people talking down to you, then why would you do the same thing to yourself? It is possible to hurt your own feelings and damage your self-esteem. One of the first traps they are taught to avoid is those that you do without realizing it. Through CBT, you learn to identify these habits, stop them, and then change that point of view.

## Problem-Solving With Depression or Anxiety

Problem-solving therapy empowers people, so they are better equipped to change the circumstances of their lives. They learn to work through challenges and take a proactive approach to their problems. Through this type of program, patients learn how to manage these issues through several core components:

**Addressing the Problem:** There are many approaches that people can take when they deal with a problem. Some will naturally be more submissive in the decision-making phase, others will apply avoidance techniques, and others will be more aggressive. Whatever strategy one takes, the treatment will focus on the developing thoughts and attitudes one applies to solve their particular problems. It will work to identify certain weaknesses and address those with cognitive steps and techniques.

**Defining the Problem:** The next step is to define exactly what the problem is so they have a clear understanding of what they are dealing with. For example, a client may see that they are constantly under stress while at work. The first conclusion might be that they are dealing with anxiety. However, other factors may be at the root of the anxiety. They may not be assertive enough on the job and as a result, are allowing people to overburden them with additional work. They may not be setting boundaries, so people do not know their limits, and this is adding to their stress level.

**Developing Strategies to Help Them Cope:** Together, they work with the therapist to outline very specific steps that will help them to change their behavior and provide a number of possible solutions to the problem. By taking into consideration a wide variety of possibilities that will work, they may feel more empowered and actually begin to believe that they can work it out.

**Execution:** Finally, when they have broken down their goals into smaller easy-to-achieve steps, they are better capable of taking the necessary action to solve the problem. As they progress through the different steps, they will gain confidence and are more likely to follow the plan and successfully solve their problems.

There have been many studies that have definitively shown that this type of therapy can be a very useful form of therapy on its own. However, it can be even more effective when it is included in a full CBT treatment plan, yielding even better results.

## CBT with Sleep Disorders

Often, people who struggle with sleep disorders have an extremely difficult time dealing with life in general. With a lack of sleep, they will naturally suffer from low energy, and when their energy is low, they are likely to also have poor nutrition. Poor nutrition contributes to brain fogginess, and in the end, they are caught up in a vicious cycle that is difficult for them to break free from. CBT can help them to get to the root cause of their sleep disorder and correct the wayward thoughts that are interrupting their ability to sleep.

Insomnia, a common sleep disorder that affects many people, has been treated very effectively through CBT. The condition makes it hard to fall asleep and even more difficult to stay asleep once you do.

CBT-1, the form of therapy used for sleep disorders, is a structured program that helps you to replace those intrusive thoughts with the kind of habits that will be more conducive to getting good sleep. The right treatment used for your sleep disorder will depend on a variety of factors.

**Stimulus Control Therapy:** This form of therapy focuses on removing the factors that may be contributing to your inability to sleep. These could include setting up routines that will support a better bedtime routine, one that is more conducive to sleep. It may involve setting up a consistent time to go to bed and wake up, avoiding naps, and restricting the use of the bed for anything other than sleeping and sex. No eating, watching TV or talking on the phone while in bed.

**Sleep Restriction:** This treatment would prevent you from being in bed for too long a time without sleeping. If you're in bed for more than 20 minutes without sleeping, it can add to your sleep deprivation. With sleep restriction, the amount of time you spend in the bed is shortened to only when you can sleep. Once you have developed a healthy sleep period, this time can be extended until you reach a point where you can sleep through the night.

**Sleep Hygiene:** This will get rid of those negative habits that interrupt sleep. Smoking, too much caffeine late in the day, consuming too much alcohol, or lack of exercise can all be part of the problem. CBT therapy can help you to reduce or eliminate those habits so that you can more easily relax before bedtime.

**Sleep Environment Improvement:** This treatment focuses on habits that create a positive sleep environment. Strategies to keep the room dark, quiet, and at the right temperature can be very effective in teaching a patient to relax.

**Passive Awakeness:** This focuses on avoiding any attempt to fall asleep. Interestingly enough, worrying about not being able to sleep can contribute to one's inability to sleep. Learning how to not worry about it allows the body to relax so you can drift off to sleep more easily.

**Biofeedback:** Once a person is aware of how his biological functions are operating, they can learn how to manipulate them. Many of these factors can interrupt one's sleep. A person's heart rate, tension in their muscles, or body temperature can all interfere with their regular sleep patterns. Learning how to mentally adjust these and other biological elements can put your body into a more comfortable state where sleep will come easily.

Whether your sleep disorder is mild or extreme, using CBT-1 can help all sorts of problems. Even if the cause of the problem is physical, as in cases of chronic pain, or mental, as in cases of anxiety and depression, the problems tend to go away once the right kind of therapy is undertaken, all without negative side effects. It will require consistent practice and applications, but the longer you stick with it, the better the end results will be.

# Chapter 3: Common Causes of Mood Disorders

When you first start Cognitive Behavioral Therapy, one of the first things you will have to do is to identify the root cause of your dysfunction. In nearly every case, the problem lies in your automatic thoughts. These are at the heart of the theory behind this type of treatment.

Automatic thoughts are known to pop into your mind without any effort. They are the brain's means of processing all of the information it is receiving from the environment. These thoughts do not represent any type of fact about the situation that it is processing, which is why they can cause so much damage. The type of automatic thoughts that appear immediately after dealing with a specific situation can be referred to as your "instinctive" response. They appear so quickly that there is literally no time to reason on the situation or apply logic, so relying on them to make decisions is often the reason why a person would display dysfunctional behavior.

In your first session with the therapist, you will learn to recognize your dysfunctional thoughts. Likely, you will backtrack from a specific experience in order to identify the actual thought that triggered your negative emotion. You should pay close attention to any thoughts that cause you to have a reflex change in mood in response to it. These are the dangerous thoughts that are connected to what you truly believe about something.

A good example of this may be how you react when you watch someone speaking in public. Your knee-jerk reaction to what is said is a reflection of what you truly believe about that situation. If there is a great deal of approval from the audience but you don't like it, your mind won't take the time to contemplate his words. If you are applying your feelings to yourself, your thoughts might reflect a general negativity about yourself. "People will never respond to me like that," or "I wish

I was as happy as he is." These personal negative reflections are labeled as "dysfunctional automatic thoughts." These beliefs will trigger equally negative feelings that are, in turn, triggering certain behaviors you want to change.

To address these thoughts through CBT, you will first have to figure out if your negative thought patterns are caused by a physical imbalance in your system. There are several things that could tell if you are physically out of balance.

## Chemical Imbalances

There is quite a bit of dispute about whether chemical imbalances are a real cause of mental disorders or not. It was once believed that chemical imbalances are the result of too much of some chemicals or too little being produced in the brain. These chemicals, called neurotransmitters, are used to aid in the communication between the neurons of the brain. You may have heard of many of them: dopamine, serotonin, and norepinephrine are just a few. It was generally understood in the world of psychiatry that mental disorders like depression and anxiety are usually the result of these chemicals being out of balance in the brain.

These types of disorders can be extremely complex, and finding a definitive answer to your problem is not always easy. However, a good way to assess whether or not you're dealing with these types of imbalances is by looking at the symptoms.

- Feeling sad, worthless, or empty
- Tendency to overeat
- Loss of appetite
- Inability to sleep
- Sleeping too much
- Feeling restless
- Irritable

- A constant feeling of dread
- Listless
- Not wanting to associate with others
- Lacking empathy
- Feeling numb all over
- Extreme mood swings
- Inability to concentrate
- Suicidal thoughts
- Thoughts of hurting others
- Inability to perform normal everyday activities
- Hearing voices that are not there
- Substance abuse

While we don't know the exact cause of these imbalances, many researchers believe that it could be a combination of genetics, our environment, and social influences on our lives. It is even unclear how these are able to affect us and create mental disorders. What we do know is that even if you do have a chemical imbalance, it is not the end of the situation. By applying the techniques of CBT, it is possible to change to more positive behaviors, which can, in time, correct them.

**Dopamine:** The brain uses dopamine to control both your movements and your emotional responses. When it is balanced properly, it is an essential component for physical and mental wellbeing. It also helps facilitate important brain functions like your mood, your ability to sleep, how you learn, concentration, motor control, and even the ability to remember things. If you are low in dopamine, you are likely to feel:

- Muscle cramps
- Tremors

- Aches and pains
- Stiffness in the muscles
- Have difficulty keep your balance
- Constipation
- Trouble eating or swallowing
- An unexplainable weight loss or weight gain
- Gastroesophageal reflux disease
- Trouble sleeping
- Low energy
- Poor concentration
- Excessive fatigue
- Unmotivated
- Extreme sadness or hopelessness
- Poor self-esteem
- Anxiety
- Suicidal thoughts
- Low libido
- A lack of self-awareness

A dopamine deficiency may be linked to a number of mental health disorders. It may not be the direct cause, but it can certainly contribute to the severity of the problem.

**Serotonin:** While your body mostly uses serotonin in the digestive system, it can have an effect on every part of your body including your emotions. It can also be found in the blood platelets and in various parts of the central nervous system. It is made from tryptophan, an amino acid found in common foods like nuts, cheese, and red meat. When you have a deficiency of serotonin, it can trigger anxiety or depressive mood disorders.

Because it can be found throughout the body, it can have a major impact on everything from your emotions to your motor skills. It is the body's natural way of keeping the mood stable. It also helps with eating, digesting foods, and allowing us to relax enough so we can sleep. When you have a good balance of serotonin, your body can:

- Fight off depression
- Control levels of anxiety
- Heal wounds better
- Maintain good bone health

You will also find that you are:

- Happier
- Emotionally stable
- Calmer
- Less anxious
- Able to concentrate better

If your serotonin levels are too high, it could be a sign of carcinoid syndrome, a condition that causes tumors in the small intestine, bronchial tubes, appendix, or the colon. Your doctor could determine your serotonin levels through a simple blood test. Symptoms of a serotonin deficiency are:

- Poor memory
- Signs of aggression
- Low or depressed mood
- Anxiety
- Cravings for sweet or starchy foods
- Insomnia
- Low self-esteem

You are equally at risk of major health problems if your serotonin levels are too high or too low, so it is very important to keep a good balance to protect not just your physical health but your mental health as well.

**Other Imbalances:** There are other chemicals in the brain that can have an effect on your moods and emotions. However, as we now understand how the brain works, it is important to realize that there is still an ongoing debate as to what extent these imbalances actually cause or affect the moods and emotions.

It should be a foregone conclusion that no person is born with these anxiety disorders. Whether the imbalances are a result of one's genetic make-up or are from the environment, it is clear that there is only one way that we know of to fix it. We have already learned that habits and behaviors are developed by using the neural pathways in the brain to send signals back and forth. Since these chemicals are responsible for facilitating that communication, it only stands to reason that the best way to treat imbalances is to strengthen those connections.

Because it focuses on those automatic thoughts, even if there is a chemical imbalance, it can be reversed by regular practice of the routine steps and strategies a patient will learn while working through the steps of CBT.

# Chapter 4: Understanding Your Moods and the Way You Think

Understanding your mood and the way you think is not easy. As you analyze a particular situation where you have been feeling those negative emotions, you have to start with a serious self-analysis. Your goal is to figure out exactly what kind of thoughts and feelings you have lying just underneath the surface. You can do this by asking yourself some very pointed questions:

- What was I doing when I began to feel that way?
- Where was I?
- Is this the only place where I feel like this?
- What was my behavior like before and after this episode?
- What hidden beliefs do I have that are showing right now?
- What causes me to intensify those feelings?
- Who was I with?
- Am I the same with everyone or just certain people?

An honest answer to these types of questions can be very revealing. For example, a person may start to feel depressed when he is alone and away from other people. These types of questions help you to get to exactly why you have experienced those sudden mood changes. If you're a person that suddenly feels awkward and ashamed when you're in the gym, you may be harboring hidden beliefs in relation to your body image. If you start to feel negative emotions while out in public, it could mean that you have serious concerns about your abilities to perform in front of strangers.

After doing this type of exercise, most people are surprised when they learn so much about themselves this way. It can be alarming to discover that their automatic thoughts, which are often just fleeting in the mind, can have such power, triggering emotions unexpectedly as if they just came on without warning. Usually, these thoughts reveal a very specific issue and once you know what it is, you can now direct your energy to that particular thought process.

## How to Diagnose Your Negative Thought Patterns

As you get started working your way through this stage of therapy, you must realize that no two people will have the exact same disorder. While they may have been diagnosed with the same label, your personal experience will be very different from someone else, because you bring to it your own personal body of experiences.

Even finding the answers to questions like the ones listed above are not easy to do. You may have to get a frank viewpoint from someone close to you and whom you can trust to get the ball rolling. Some complete the entire first session without learning what is at the heart of their problem. However, they will have learned how to start trying to think differently about their experiences.

This is not to be surprising. Most of us have gotten pretty good at hiding some of those negatives that permeate our lives every day and have done so for years. It's not likely that everything is going to come out in the first wash. Still, if you persist in this type of self-analysis, there is a very good chance that you will be able to identify many of the tricks and tactics you have created to cover up your true feelings about certain things.

As you go through this process, don't be afraid to look at every aspect of your life and not just in the obvious areas. It is quite often that the real trigger has little or no direct connection to where your thinking went awry. For example, you may be having a communication problem with your spouse. He or she may think you are distant, uncommunicative, or just has lost interest in the relationship. However, if you're dealing with a hidden anxiety or depression that started many years prior, it may still be affecting you and causing you to separate from your partner.

Imagine it this way. You are a child and you have a close and dear friend who died of a sudden illness. Your relationship was strong, and you were always very happy when with that person. However, their death suddenly left a huge void in your life. On the surface, you were able to eventually get over it and move on, but that pain was never clearly addressed. Now, in a relationship, you are afraid to commit that way to another person.

This kind of hidden pain could be what is causing those automatic thoughts that are firing in your brain.

- I can't commit to another person, they will leave me.
- I can't go through losing someone again in my life.
- It's not worth it. Everybody is going to die anyway.

A past loss may have been the real reason you don't trust or are afraid to communicate with your spouse. People die, friends move away, jobs are lost, and a myriad of other conditions could be behind the reason for your automatic thoughts. If you were a child when it happened, it is quite possible your grief was either not recognized or considered unimportant in a world where everyone else is in grief too. However, being able to learn the hidden secrets that are triggering those automatic thoughts can give you great insight on where they come from and why they are resurfacing. As a result, you have a basis for addressing the issue now and correcting those thoughts from a more realistic position.

Now, this may seem strange in light of what we said earlier; that a CBT therapist does not reach back into our past to find the root cause of a problem. This is true, however, as you begin to recognize these automatic thoughts, it is only a small step to making the connection between your past and the present.

Once you are able to identify those thoughts, there are several ways you can deal with them.

- If you feel the thought is indicative of a larger issue, you can choose to put all your energies into correcting that thought.
- If you feel that there is another problem that better identifies the issue, you can choose to focus on the two thoughts together.
- If you discover that there are other issues that are beginning to surface, you can put the initial thought aside and focus on the bigger and most important issues first.

After you have uncovered these hidden thoughts, the next step is to analyze each thought and rate them as to how important they are. If one thought seems to produce intense feelings in one way or another, it is likely the one that has the biggest impact.

Sometimes, it can be difficult to separate the different thoughts in your mind. In that case, it is helpful to keep a notepad nearby and write down the thoughts as they appear. As you write down each thought, make sure to also take note of what was happening when it occurred and the feelings it evoked. If you do this over a period of time (perhaps a week), you'll begin to notice a definite pattern emerge.

There are several different categories of automatic thoughts, and by journaling them as they happen, the patterns that emerge will help you to classify the type of thoughts you're having. Below is a list of some of the most common beliefs that many people develop that can trigger negative emotions.

- All or nothing: A person who believes everything is either black or white with no middle ground or gray area.
- Catastrophizing: A belief that every situation will produce the worst results.

- Discounting Positives: The belief that all positive experiences are false.

- Emotional Reasoning: Allowing one's negative feelings about a situation to be the deciding voice in their head.

- Jumping to Conclusions: Automatically concluding negative results for a situation with any evidence to back up assumptions.

- Labeling: The act of giving negative labels to ourselves or to other people. Calling yourself a loser or a failure rather than making the effort to change the quality you don't like.

- Magnification/Minimization: Putting a lot of emphasis on anything bad and downgrading anything good. Really stressing out about a mistake but not willing to accept compliments or acknowledge achievements.

- Negative Bias: Seeing only the bad in any situation and dwelling on the negative, despite the fact that there are many positives.

- Overgeneralizations: Using a single negative experience to represent every other similar event.

- Personalization: Believing that negative comments or actions from others are about you or believing that you are the cause of a bad event even when you had no connection with it.

- Should/Must statements: Having expectations based on what you believe should be done. These often stem from distorted perceptions of what others may believe about you and are likely not in the realm of reality. This could cause you to feel guilty for not meeting these abstract standards or often excessively high expectations.

Likely, as you read through this list, some of these dysfunctional automatic thoughts popped out at you. All of us have them from time to time, but if you think they are interfering with the progression in your life, then these should be the ones that you should focus your CBT exercises on.

# Intrusive Thoughts

In our minds, we have many thoughts throughout the course of a single day. It is estimated that each of us has between 50-70,000 thoughts in a single 24-hour period. Most of them, we are able to quickly dismiss as insignificant and unimportant. But there are those disturbing thoughts that seem to get stuck in our brain and no matter what we do; we can't seem to get rid of them. They make us feel sad, frightened, and sometimes, even sick and can create a great deal of turmoil in our emotions.

The fact that they are so intrusive and they seem to camp out in our head can cause us even more distress; some to the point where they interfere with our regular routines and activities causing us to feel ashamed, guilty, or afraid. Anyone suffering from an anxiety disorder like OCD or PTSD can quickly relate to the kind of damage an intrusive thought like these can do.

These thoughts are always unpleasant and can even make you feel repulsed. They can include acts of violence, inappropriate sexual acts, or extreme criminal behavior. Those in relation to anxiety could be an excessive worry about future events or threats. Strategies learned through CBT can help to reduce their frequency and even help to lessen the extremes that they may take. Addressing these feelings would be a good way to start getting rid of them.

## Examples of Some Intrusive Thoughts

- Unwanted sexual fantasies involving a child, animal, or another person close to you
- Unwanted sexual thoughts involving someone you work with but are not really attracted to.
- Imagining yourself committing a violent criminal act
- Fear that you will say the wrong thing in public

- Doubts about your religion or thoughts of doing something forbidden
- Doubts about your inability to do well on an exam you know you have prepared for
- Recurring thoughts about getting a rare disease
- Fear of death
- Repeated memories about something humiliating that happened in your childhood
- Repeated memories about a violent experience you had in the past

It is important to know at this point, that having intrusive thoughts is not indicative of a disorder. Everyone has them at one point or another. According to the *Journal of Obsessive-Compulsive Disorders*, 94% of people in the world have intrusive thoughts. It is one of the most common mental activities that we all have. What is different in those who have anxiety or depressive disorders is our reaction to those thoughts.

When you are healthy and your mental state is balanced, you are able to dismiss those thoughts and they won't upset you. When you struggle with those thoughts, it is because you have already associated a great deal of importance to them, which is an indication that you have an internal belief that they are true and accurate. In such cases, your mind starts to create a full narrative about those thoughts and conjure up its own implications about what kind of behavior you should display or what your future actions should be.

To counteract these thoughts, one of the first things you need to do is analyze them, so you can convince yourself that they are NOT true. This is especially important when you are dealing with some of the above thoughts that may be violent or otherwise inappropriate. It does not mean that you really want to do those things. If you continue to accept these things as true, then it can saddle you with an immeasurable sense of guilt and shame, which could cause you even more problems.

If you're struggling with these types of intrusive thoughts, then take some of the following steps to apply some CBT-based strategies to combat them.

## Identifying Your Triggers for Anxiety and Stress

It is one thing to know what your problem is and another thing entirely to identify what is triggering the symptoms you're experiencing. Finding these triggers can be quite complicated as it is most likely due to a combination of factors including environmental, physical, and genetics. Even so, there are some events or personal experiences that may trigger certain forms of anxiety or, at the very least, make them much worse.

So, whether you're dealing with symptoms of anxiety, depression, or stress as a result of a genetic factor that you have no control over, the condition can actually deepen as a result of certain events or experiences you are having in your day-to-day life. These events, emotions, and experiences are called triggers.

These triggers can vary from one person to the next. However, in most cases, you're likely responding to several triggers at one time. It may seem, on the surface, that your reaction to a given situation comes completely out of nowhere, but in most cases, there is always something there, just underneath the surface. So, while it may be uncomfortable to do, it is important to root out your personal triggers, so you can take proactive steps in managing them. Below are some of the most common triggers that many people have.

**Health Issues:** Often, your own health may be playing a part in increasing your anxiety or depression. Diseases such as cancer or another type of chronic illness can trigger anxiety or even make it worse. Just getting a diagnosis of a disease like cancer can immediately evoke powerfully negative emotions that can be very difficult to combat.

To counteract this kind of trigger, you need to take a proactive approach by working together with your doctor and even discussing it with a therapist as they can give you strategies to help you manage your emotions as you go through your treatment.

**Medications:** The intrusive thoughts and negative emotions may be the result of the medication you're taking. While there is always a risk with certain prescription drugs of generating negative thoughts, even over-the-counter medications have been known to trigger anxiety and/or depression. This is due to the active ingredients that are working on your system. If you are able to dismiss these thoughts as a result of the medication, then great, but many people do not realize that the feelings they generate can trigger a number of side effects that could increase your level of anxiety.

Common medications that have been known to trigger anxiety/depression:

- birth control pills
- cold/flu medications to treat a cough and congestion
- weight loss medications

While for most people the symptoms will be non-existent or minimal, for those who have anxiety and depression disorders, these could pose a real problem. If after taking any medication, you find the intrusive thoughts are increasing or are causing negative emotions, speak with your doctor and get him/her to help you find an acceptable alternative.

**Caffeine:** Believe it or not, many people are addicted to caffeine, not realizing that it can be a very strong trigger for anxiety. Research has shown that people who are already susceptible to panic disorders or social anxiety disorders will be even more sensitive to the negative effects of caffeine.

To combat this, one of the best things you can do is to reduce or eliminate the amount of caffeine you consume and substitute it with other options for the stimulation you need.

**Your Diet:** Believe it or not, your diet can be a major contributing factor to your mental stability. Skipping meals, especially, can have a negative impact on your mental state. When you miss a meal, it causes your blood sugar levels to drop, which can trigger anxiety along with a host of other symptoms including that jittery feeling, nervousness, or agitation.

The best way to counteract this problem is to eat regularly and make sure that you have a diet that is balanced so that you get an adequate amount of nutrients in your system. The old rule that you must eat 3-5 meals a day is no longer encouraged. However, you need to make sure that your diet consists of enough nutrients to sustain you on a daily basis to prevent a drop in blood sugar.

**Negativity:** Nothing happens in our body unless it first happens in our mind, including anxiety. Your brain is the control center for your entire body so when you have anxiety, your self-talk can have a major impact on how you function. If you tend to be negative in your conversation or you are known for using a lot of negativity in reference to yourself, it can create a perpetual negative outlook on everything you do. Learn to use more positive expressions in your conversation and your feelings will soon follow. If you find this difficult, consider working with a therapist for a while until you learn to change your automatic conversation to a more positive and up-building form of self-talk.

**Financial Problems:** Debt can be a painful burden to undergo. Constant worry about not having enough or finding ways to save money can trigger a great deal of anxiety. While you may not be able to change your circumstances immediately, learning to manage these types of triggers can help to ease a lot of your intrusive thoughts. Working with a therapist can help guide you to a process that could help to get your mind to relax more.

**Public Situations:** Often, public events that include a lot of strangers can make one feel uncomfortable. The pressure of having to interact feels like walking through unfamiliar territory and can trigger many anxious feelings.

Worries about such occasions can be reduced by asking a trusted friend to accompany you so you won't feel like you're on your own. If your anxiety about these things is particularly intense, consider learning some coping mechanisms from a professional therapist so you are better equipped to managing them.

**Conflict:** Conflict in any form can be very stressful. Whether it is a relationship problem or a disagreement at work, these can trigger some of the worse anxiety you can deal with. If this is becoming a particularly stressful area for you, consider learning some conflict resolution strategies to learn better ways to control your feelings when conflicts arise.

**Stress:** We all face stress on a daily basis, but some of us get a bigger dose of it than others. Daily stress, when it is intense and constant, can trigger extreme anxiety symptoms along with other health problems. When under stress, you are likely picking up other habits that will contribute to your anxiety levels. Habits like over drinking, skipping meals, or insomnia will only intensify the anxiety.

Learning to first identify these habits and a few coping mechanisms will help you to handle them better so that they aren't allowed to overwhelm you.

**Public Events/Performances:** Situations that require you to speak or perform in public can be extremely stressful. Whether it is speaking up at a business meeting or competing at a special event, the stress can trigger all sorts of negative emotions and behaviors.

Try working along with a trusted friend or relative with some positive reinforcement to help you prepare and feel more comfortable beforehand. Regular practice with people you trust and even having them along with you for support can help you to feel more confident and relaxed.

**Your Own Personal Triggers:** It may be that you have triggers that are unique to you. These may not be so easy to identify. They could be something as simple as a smell that triggers something in your mind, the sounds of a song, the resemblance of a place or any number of things that can bring back a memory of a past traumatic event. This is common with people who suffer from PTSD. The triggers could be any number of things in their environment.

If you can identify these triggers, you can then take the next step to address them. Since these personal triggers are not likely to be those experienced by others, you will have to do a little bit of soul searching to uncover them. To help you find them, try these tips:

- Start keeping a journal where you take note of when your anxiety or depression is heightened. Record your thoughts and your feelings that occur at the same time. For example, answer the 5 W's (who, what, when, where, and why). After a while, you'll be able to see a certain pattern begin to emerge that will give you clues to your triggers.

- Be honest with yourself. Negative self-talk stems from a poor assessment of your true values and qualities. As long as you stay within that negative mode, it will be difficult to uncover the triggers to your anxiety and depression. Don't just accept the first thing that comes in your head. Be patient and be willing to look a little deeper into your life (past and present) to identify how they are making you feel.

- If the above two tips don't work, consider spending some time with a therapist. Even with all the effort you put out, some triggers have been so well-hidden that no matter what you do, it will be hard to pull out. Working with a professional can make it easier and take a lot of the pressure off of you.

Once you know and have identified your triggers, you have accomplished the first step in Cognitive Behavioral Therapy. Now, you can make a list of the problems you're facing and choose the ones you'd like to address and you're ready to move on to the next step in CBT.

# Chapter 5: How it Treats Mood Disorders

During your first week of CBT, after you've identified the major problems you want to address, you'll have to go into setting goals for yourself. You know the type of anxiety and depression you're experiencing. Now, you need to work on a system for addressing these issues.

## Practical Applications of CBT

Since no two forms of anxiety or depressive disorders are the same, there is no single way to deal with the challenges that each individual may face. Even those with the same diagnosis will have a different approach to their treatment. This means that before setting your goals, you need to have a pretty clear idea of what your specific problem is and what challenges you are facing. Once your unique situation is understood, then you can determine what kinds of changes are needed.

Generally, this is done at the first meeting with the therapist. You will be asked a number of questions that, at first, may not seem too important. For example, the therapist is likely to ask, *"Why are you here?"* Or in the case of trying CBT through the pages of this book, ask yourself, *"Why are you reading this book?"* This will prompt you to do an internal examination of your motivation for wanting to try CBT.

You might also spend some time determining what your strengths are. While you are looking at CBT to solve many of your problems, you will use your strengths as a tool to combat your struggles. There are several ways you can uncover your strengths. These are usually the things that people tend to recognize and admire about you, those qualities that others appreciate about you. Maybe, at this point, you don't see these qualities in yourself, but others do, so consider talking to someone close to you to find out just what they see in you that can be useful.

Next, you will need to take a step back and examine how your life is going at the moment. But don't just do a surface look at the conditions. Take extra notice of how the anxiety/depression is affecting you. There are several different aspects that you can examine closely.

- **Relationships:** Relationships often affect our overall health probably more than anything else. When your marriage is on the skids, it usually means that you're not satisfied with your life in general and that attitude can lead to some very negative thoughts. However, if you have a life full of positive relationships and full of supportive people, your outlook on life will have a more positive spin.

  As you examine the relationships, look at how your anxiety/depression is affecting them. For example, you may have a supportive relationship, but is your depression causing you to pull away and not spend as much time with them. Your anxiety may be causing you to live your life on a short fuse, constantly snapping at them or keeping you angry and on edge all the time.

  Don't just look at a relationship with your spouse or significant other but consider how it is playing out with your parents, siblings, friends, children, and even coworkers. Determine what is good in your relationships and what is not. How do you feel about the people who have moved out of your life (either by moving away, a death, or an unresolved disagreement)?

  Finally, think about your relationships that are affecting your anxiety/depression. Are they making you more anxious or more depressed? Take note of the answer to these questions because you will have to face them later.

- **Physical Health:** Next, take some time to analyze your overall health. Here, you want to consider your eating habits, the amount of physical

140

activity you're involved in, and what substances you regularly use (alcohol, drugs, etc.) The goal here is to draw a line between your regular habits and how they are affecting you physically. These can easily affect your moods and cause anxiety or depression.

As you consider health, think about any chronic health issues you're dealing with. Conditions like high blood pressure, diabetes, asthma, or other ongoing physical challenges can create huge inroads on your mood. If you're getting more physical exercise, how are you feeling about it? Do you enjoy your regular routine or do you find it a chore; something that you just have to get done? Is there a kind of activity that you enjoy more than others or do you just not like moving at all?

Look at how much alcohol or drugs you use each day. These include prescription drugs as well as less favorable ones. If you've had a problem with substance abuse in the past, this is something that you need to give some serious thought to.

The same weight should be given to your diet. If you are a stress eater, you are likely eating foods that are hampering your ability to function. You may not even realize that you're eating these foods. Another concern should be if you're eating enough or overeating. These habits will affect your weight, which could have a direct impact on your own self-image, self-esteem, and self-respect; all of which will affect your moods.

Sleep also can affect your physical health. If you're not getting enough or you're getting too much, it can have an impact on your daily routine. It can keep you from getting the kind of movement you need and even the kind of foods you eat. Look at any external factors that could be affecting your normal sleep routine: pets, partners, work, kids, etc.

All of us need to have some downtime. If we allow our lives to encroach on that time, our activity level will suffer. There are probably many things you'd like to be doing and many things you'd rather not be doing. If your activity level is too high, chances are that you haven't had much time to relax and destress. You may also not have had any time to do the kind of things you enjoy doing like sports, hobbies, travels, etc. You can be highly active and still not have time to do the things you enjoy.

You will take this week to examine your entire life to see how these factors and others are affecting your mood. Afterward, go back over everything you've noted and see how it affects you. First, look at how it has affected your life and your mood in the past, but then take some time to meditate on them. Note what negative emotions come out as you're doing this review. Common feelings that emerge just talking about these things include anxiety, joy, sorry, overwhelm, sad, melancholy, etc.

## Setting Goals

With a better understanding of the problems you're coping with, it'll be much easier to set specific goals for you to start working towards. In CBT, goals need to be very specific, something that is measurable and within reach. You need to concentrate on the type of changes that will actually be meaningful to your life and that you feel you can reasonably achieve within a short amount of time.

It is important to not be vague at this point. Remember that CBT has a time limit. Whether the program you are on is six weeks or ten, your goals should reflect where you reasonably expect to be at that point. So, goals like "I want to be happier" or "I want to stop worrying so much," are not specific enough to maintain your motivation for the duration of the program.

Instead, your goals should have very defined parameters. "I want to be able to get up on time every day," or "I want to find time to do something I enjoy." Your goals need to relate directly to the specific problems you are facing. "I want to voice my opinion more in employee meetings."

You want to avoid making grand goals that will require a major commitment; instead, focus on something that is well within your ability to achieve in a one, two, or three-week period. When you make large goals that are far out of your scope of ability, try to set a series of smaller goals that will help you to reach the larger ones at a later date. You can have these larger expectations set for years later, but it's best to break them up into smaller steps with each one taking you closer and closer to what you ultimately want to achieve. As you progress through the program, you will develop a more balanced view of yourself, which will help you to improve in your ability to accomplish more.

## Building Self-Esteem

When you are suffering from low self-esteem, CBT can be very practical in helping you to identify the source of your negative thoughts, and how it influences your behavior. By incorporating these strategies, those dealing with self-esteem issues can work their way towards a healthier lifestyle.

Because CBT works on your personal perception of yourself, the techniques learned will help you understand how your mind works to create its own meanings in your experiences, and then teach you how to reframe your negative views and alter them by focusing on building a more positive structure of thoughts to rely on.

Throughout your sessions, you may learn techniques like:

- **Cognitive Restructuring:** where you focus on thought patterns and their sources. By regular reflection on these patterns, you will learn how to analyze your method of judgment and start reshaping your perception into more realistic possibilities.

- **Behavioral Activation:** where you identify those situations that cause you discomfort or make you afraid. By engaging in this technique, you are encouraged to step out of your comfort zone and gradually learn how to insert yourself into new situations.

- **Assertiveness Training:** through assertiveness training, you learn to reclaim your self-confidence. Through this, you are motivated to step out of your area of comfort and assert yourself in various areas where you can build up your self-confidence.

- **Social Skills Training:** through this form of therapy, you learn to work on improving social skills. It may include learning how you interpret and analyze many of the social situations you may have to interact with. Since low self-esteem comes from a negative perception of interactions with others, learning how to interact in a variety of social environments will make you aware of how your mind processes these situations and redirects them into a more positive direction.

Anyone suffering from a low self-esteem can learn how their thoughts relate to their actions and how to reflect on their impact and work to redirect them in a healthier and more positive lifestyle.

# Verbal Self-Talk

We talk to ourselves all the time, but when you have negative self-talk, it can be very damaging. We often say things to ourselves that we would never dare say to anyone else. Our stress does not just come from external input, but our own emotional makeup can significantly add to it. In fact, studies have shown that our emotional makeup can actually cause so much stress in our bodies that it changes our physical make-up. Negative self-talk can cause changes in a number of health issues including:

- Diarrhea/constipation
- Muscle tension and pain
- Ulcers
- Headaches
- Insomnia
- Teeth grinding
- High blood pressure
- Cold hands/feet

All of these, in addition to our anxiety and depression, we may be suffering from. Chronic stress depletes the body of the essential chemicals that it needs to function properly. When we lack these essentials, we leave ourselves open for a number of illnesses. However, it is possible for us to change the way we respond to external and internal elements and develop a more healing environment that will give us better health.

It starts with changing how we talk to ourselves. CBT can teach you how to control your negative reactions to different things by teaching you different ways to interpret your personal experiences. So, rather than berating yourself for a simple mistake, you could remind yourself of all the times you did things well.

This helps to reduce feelings of guilt, shame, and anxiety that are eroding our mental and physical health. By changing these negative thought patterns into positive affirmations, you will find your mental state will gradually begin to turn into another direction.

## Counter Negative and Angry Feelings

Anger is a unique negative feeling. Unlike other negative emotions like sadness, guilt, or disgust, anger can also have a positive side to it, so all anger is not bad. Sometimes referred to as the moral emotion, it often appears in cases where morals are brought into question. Values like justice, fairness, and respect are at its core.

There may be times, however, when you may not be able to make the connection between the root of your anger and its actual cause. You may, for example, feel you are angry at one person or another, but the cause may be from an entirely different source. This makes anger a sort of an enigma. We know that it usually precedes aggression, so it pays to address this issue as soon as possible. Negative anger can be treated with several different approaches to CBT. In fact, studies show that in as little as 8-12 weeks, there have been some very promising results. Techniques such as problem-solving, relaxation strategies, and enhanced communication skills have all been very effective in helping people to handle their anger better.

## Dealing With Feelings of Guilt

Everyone has to deal with guilt at some point. No matter who we are, holding onto the wrongs we've done in the past is probably the most common reason why people don't move forward. Most of it comes from having to deal with the consequences of the poor decisions we've made, but the feeling that one act can stop us from moving on with our lives can be crippling.

No matter what has been done in the past, since it is not possible to do those things over in a different way, when negative results occur, the guilt that results can become like a life sentence that you impose upon yourself. Getting rid of that guilt on your own can sometimes feel impossible.

Through CBT, you can be guided through looking at that past event and learn how to see it through fresh eyes; eyes that can see the situation from different angles. One particular technique applied is a technique called The Blame Pie. This tool helps you to see just how much control you had over the negative situation and that, in most cases, you were not totally responsible. It looks at each individual involved in the incident and divides the blame according to their contribution to the event. As each person is assigned a percentage of the blame, it literally lifts much of the weight off your shoulders.

This type of treatment, over time, can help someone to get past the weight of the responsibility they had and finally find themselves worthy of moving on to a better life.

## Counteract Hopelessness

Sometimes, depression can become so deep that a person feels completely hopeless. Because depression is the result of negative thinking, recovery from something as severe as hopelessness can be painfully slow. Even if you have positive thoughts on occasion, when you reach the point of hopelessness, you may not allow them to surface long enough to reap the effects.

Normally, in a depressed state of mind, positive emotions are often squelched with more powerful, negative thoughts like "I don't deserve to be happy," or "I know this won't last." In their minds, even when they feel good, they are unable to enjoy it because they are waiting for the ax to fall.

Through CBT, identifying the pattern of thoughts that lead to negative behavior can be changed. Once you're better able to identify these patterns, you can recognize them when they arise, freeing your mind for more positive thoughts. This can be done in several phases:

- Identifying the problem and mapping out solutions.
- Write down more positive statements that can counteract the negative thoughts.
- Actively search for new opportunities to apply positive thoughts.
- Learn to accept disappointment as a normal part of life.

# Chapter 6: Steps to Dealing with Mood Disorders and Depression

Preventing mood disorders and depression is at the heart of Cognitive Behavioral Therapy. It has a multilevel approach that starts small and builds, helping patients to change their thought processes in everything they do. With each step, they celebrate small advances that will help them to gradually get closer and closer to their goals.

The first phase of the therapy involves identifying the problem they are facing, which is generally the result of automatic and intrusive thoughts. This is a crucial phase of the therapy as it defines a starting point for the treatment needed. Without a solid knowledge of the problem, it would be difficult to target the right strategies and techniques to deal with it directly.

The second phase is a period of goal setting where they can work on where they want to be within a set timeframe. After identifying the biggest issues you may be facing, it is much easier to map out a series of steps that will help you to focus on the changes you want to make.

In phase three, you will need to identify the challenges and obstacles you will be facing that will likely get in the way of your goals. No path will be easy as you will have to deal with a variety of setbacks along the way. You can decide to use them as a roadblock preventing your progress, as an obstacle that will require you to make a detour on your path to success, or as a stepping stone used to help you to get to where you really want to be.

Phase four deals with learning how to challenge your automatic and intrusive thoughts. In this phase, patients learn how to separate reality from the exaggerated thoughts they normally have. Once these negative thoughts have been identified, they can be challenged by a series of questions that forces them to use logic to come to a more reasonable conclusion. At this point, you will need to look for factual evidence that will contradict your embedded beliefs. Once those beliefs have been identified and successfully refuted, then you can learn how to use the evidence to refute those beliefs. Over time, those beliefs will diminish and be replaced by more realistic ones.

Phase five helps with identifying even more automatic assumptions and beliefs. Now that the automatic thoughts have been identified, this phase takes it another step forward and isolates the deeper core beliefs that all people have. These are the ones that are more absolute and less flexible. They most likely have been formed in childhood, and unless changed, will stay with you throughout your life, getting reinforced over the years with each experience you have.

This phase is the best stage to address these issues because many of us are reluctant to accept that these thoughts are wrong until they have addressed their own automatic thoughts first. Challenging these beliefs is often like challenging who you are as a person because they have been deeply embedded in your mind for years to come.

Phase Six focuses on changing the behavior. Up until this point, all of the exercises are dealing with the cognitive activity in the mind. These changes can now begin to extend outward involving participation in different activities and events giving special attention to those that will deliver a more positive mood.

For those dealing with depression, participating in these activities is crucial to lifting the mood. In this phase, the focus should rely heavily on avoidance issues, depression, anxiety, and phobias. Its goal is to boost self-confidence so you are more comfortable engaging in more meaningful activities.

Phase Seven deals with the problem-solving strategies you will need. It brings home the main point of Cognitive Behavioral Therapy; convincing your mind that everything is all right and that any problems that come up, you are capable of handling. While challenging your negative thoughts and beliefs will produce good results, the ability to master the skills taught in the problem-solving phase will be the most effective in helping to ease behavioral issues.

It is important to note that each of these seven steps can help you to move closer to your goal, it will not work well for everyone. Those who are suffering from severe depression, emotional trauma, and those mental illnesses that are considered to be extreme won't likely be enough. Most of the exercises and strategies you learn in CBT can be done and practiced on your own, but if you're dealing with extreme emotional instability, then you may need more guided therapy to help you get back on the right path.

The problem-solving phase involves several steps:

1. Identify the problem and the specific elements you need to address.
2. Brainstorm possible solutions.
3. Evaluate each solution to determine the pros and cons of each.
4. Choose an optimal solution and then choose a backup.
5. Create a plan of action.
6. Execute the plan.
7. Review results and make needed adjustments.
8. If the problem is not resolved, start again at step 1.

At this phase, you will also need to review your lifestyle habits. Modifications will likely be necessary as an aid to improve how your brain processes thoughts. You will be coached in matters of sleep, eating, physical activity, and meditation.

Most people will see impressive results after applying these methods over a period of several weeks. The most common approach is to take one or two weeks to address each step. After you have successfully met the challenges of one phase, then do not hesitate to move on to the next one. Hesitation could interrupt the momentum you've developed and could cause you to lose your steam.

# Chapter 7: Multimodal Model

As you can see, there are multiple ways that CBT can help a person to counteract their negative tendencies. With their Multimodal strategy, the technique gets a little more in-depth with a closer look at the seven different aspects of the human personality.

With this model, therapy consists of using a variety of models at one time, all of which are able to be adapted to many situations because they are completely interactive. They also share the same core beliefs that an individual will use to build his thought processes on. They consist of a combination of several elements including:

- Their Biological and genetic makeup
- The Effects of their experiences
- The Sensations that exist between thoughts, feelings, and behavior
- The Imagery that occurs in their own minds, mental images both negative or positive
- Their Cognition, or the way they think whether positive or negative
- Their Interpersonal relationships with others
- Their Drugs/biology, or their physical experiences, or the use of substances

These are considered the core of this type of therapy. They can be easily identified with the acronym BASIC ID. Each of these modalities is used to help narrow down the areas in which the coaching sessions should focus on.

The beauty of the Multimodal Model is that it recognizes that different people will respond to different modalities. You may be capable of handling your problems on your own while others will rely heavily on the support of others, and others may prefer to deal with their problems through certain activities. All of these can be incorporated into the seven areas of the BASIC ID, so it is possible to focus on those strategies that will allow them to overcome the problems they face in a manner that they can feel more comfortable with.

The goal of MMD is to help the individual make the necessary changes so they can make the transition from their current state of mind to a more progressive and adaptable mental state. MMD is often used in highly complex cases of depression and performance anxiety. Those who benefit the most are experiencing negative behavior so extreme that their lives are paralyzed to the point that they are unable to move forward. Their careers and their families are already at risk or on the verge of falling apart. Some have a level of fear that has reached a climax that it has had a heavy impact on nearly all seven of the modalities, and an intervention is likely the only possible solution.

Its success can be attributed to the principle that by approaching several issues at the same time, an individual may find themselves dependent on substances or other crutches to deal with them. It could be a combination of health problems, emotional issues, and financial distress all at the same time. Each case severe enough to be addressed on their own but through MMD, it is possible to address all of these issues at the same time to facilitate a speedier recovery.

## The Seven Modalities You Should Know About

Because most psychological problems tend to be multifaceted, it is necessary to start by understanding each of the seven modalities that are actually affecting you. When you consider that many of the intervention techniques that people naturally turn to are substances, it is helpful to give even more consideration to the last modality, drugs or substances, as they will hold many techniques that can reveal your inner self. Now, let's take a closer look at each one of them to see how they are used in CBT.

**Behavior:** This aspect of MMD takes a close look at everything a patient does. This includes his habits, gestures, actions, etc. Some of his behaviors will be healthy while others will not be. Unhealthy behaviors that require particular attention could be those that are destructive, immoral, childish, illegal, impulsive, controlling, or otherwise, inappropriate.

Most patients will seek therapy because their unwanted behaviors are causing problems in their lives. Practices such as overeating, excessive drinking, hoarding, rebellion, self-mutilation, etc. are the most common. The goal is to change the behavior itself through techniques like modeling, desensitization, and aversive conditioning. The trick is that nearly all unwanted behaviors are connected to the other modalities as well, so by including this in the MMD therapy sessions, there is a much higher chance of success and the prevention of a relapse.

**Affect:** This modality refers to the inner feelings and emotions you are experiencing. Throughout the process, you may feel a wide range of emotions, but the focus of the therapy is to address the feelings you don't like. So, while you may feel happy, sad, afraid, frustrated, and bored, the sessions will likely involve the negative emotions first. Many who are seeking therapy for other reasons will often find that these emotions are at the root of their problems, even if they don't realize it in the beginning. The negative emotions are usually the underlying trigger for a wide range of other feelings that are often buried deep inside.

**Sensation:** We have five senses – sight, hearing, touch, taste, and smell, which contribute to all of our physiological experiences. Negative sensations may be butterflies in the stomach, tense muscles, physical pain, rapid heartbeat, headaches, cold hands or feet, sweating, nausea, skin crawling, and shortness of breath. Some more extreme sensations could also be hallucinations and/or illusions.

**Imagery:** This modality consists of the mental images that are built up in a person's mind. It includes things they may fantasize about, their daydreams, and their own personal self-image. Common in those who suffer from anxiety disorders, their fears are part of their imagery. They also have an excessive worry about the future. Those who struggle with depression may have images that are extremely negative and distorted, far from the reality of things. Addressing one's imagery will help them to learn how to adjust the view of the world and give them a more realistic and accurate view.

**Cognition:** Focuses on a person's beliefs, attitudes, and judgments. When thoughts are negative like limiting or distorted beliefs about something, they can contribute significantly to depression, anxiety, or any number of other disorders. When a person believes they are not worthy of something, it can have an impact on their relationships, employment, and other areas of their life, which can be very damaging.

**Interpersonal Relationships:** This takes a closer look at how they interact with others, their social skills, how they relate to people, and what kind of support system they have or is missing in their lives. A close look at their relationships will reveal if they know how to develop and maintain a lasting relationship, feel connected to others, and if they have a good balance in mental health. Those getting over a breakup, needing to resolve conflict, or are antisocial will usually find that they are also lacking in the areas of effect and cognition as well.

**Drugs, Health, Biology:** This is a combination of several things. First, it includes a person's physical health. Whether he has been fighting off any serious illnesses, his overall physical condition, any physical limitations, his age, or chronic pain are just some of the health concerns they may have. It will also include biological factors like his genetics and brain chemistry and his need for medical treatment or medications. Finally, this modality looks at his lifestyle habits including diet and nutrition, activity level, sleep and eating habits, smoking, and drug and alcohol use. Close attention needs to be considered when dealing with substances. Few people realize just how much of an impact these habits can have on your mood or mental state. By evaluating this factor carefully, you may be surprised at what it can reveal.

There are two ways these seven modalities can be assessed. It is either with a one-on-one interview with a therapist or by filling out a Multimodal Life History Inventory questionnaire. Once an assessment is determined based on the BASIC ID, then a program of therapeutic techniques and strategies can be implemented starting with the modality that represents the biggest problem.

# Chapter 8: Rational Emotive Behavioral Therapy

Rational Emotive Behavioral Therapy (REBT) places most of its importance on the thought processes of an individual. Like all other forms of CBT, it is based on the same premise that what we think triggers our feelings, which in turn, will trigger our behavior. The main idea behind REBT is to help those people who view their personal experiences in a negative way. However, they do not address the experience directly. Instead, the behavior is adjusted based on how they "perceived" the experience.

Through REBT, patients are taught how to challenge their own beliefs and replace them with a more accurate line of reasoning. It targets the inner beliefs, so they can deal with their experiences in a more realistic way. When successful, it can be very powerful, changing not just the way one thinks but also their perception of life in general.

REBT works because it recognizes that logic is not always an effective part of the human psyche. Even with logic, it is not always the best way to solve problems. Computers operate entirely on logic to perform their functions; they absorb data, analyze it, and using logic determine an acceptable output. The human brain, however, processes information differently, often without the use of logic. Therefore, some of their conclusions can be far removed from reality.

The focus of Rational Emotive Therapy is to teach people to think in a more logical manner. It works to break down the instinctual thinking process by using logical reasoning to interfere with the irrational assumptions they are making. Once these irrational thoughts have been replaced with more positive ones, it will start to filter down and change the inappropriate behavior to actions that are more positive.

No matter what negative thought a person may have, its roots are often deep within an unrealistic world. To combat this type of reasoning, REBT applies something called the ABCDE model of thinking.

## A: Activating Event

An inciting event is identified which triggers the irrational belief. This could be any number of negative experiences including an argument with someone, a car accident, or the loss of a job. It is the trauma of this event that compels the mind to create a new irrational thought or belief.

## B: The Belief

Once the belief has been created, the mind will automatically revisit it every time a similar negative event occurs. Each time the mind goes back to the belief, it is reinforced causing the person to get stuck in a spiral of negative behavior without ever really understanding why it happened in the first place.

## C: Consequences

The belief will trigger the consequences of their irrational thoughts. Some consequences could be emotional as in the case of guilt or shame, while others could be behavioral as in overeating or some form of substance abuse. The underlying emotions for these behaviors could be depression, lack of self-confidence, or hostility.

## D: Dispute

The dispute phase of the program is when you learn to challenge that belief system and see it as irrational. You begin to recognize it as the root of your problems. At this stage, you learn to argue with your subconscious mind and dispute your negative beliefs. You will be asked to come up with convincing proof that will successfully contradict your imprinted way of thinking.

# E: Effect

You could also call this phase reinforcement. Once you have had your internal debate and successfully convinced yourself that your irrational belief is wrong, more positive behaviors will be much easier to come by. You'll feel a stronger self-esteem, you'll be bolder, or you'll just feel a lot better overall.

In most cases, REBT can be done without the aid of a therapist. This model can help anyone get to the root of their negative behavior and arm them with the tools they need to change. It motivates people to look deeply at how their thoughts are developed and how to apply rationale to their beliefs and replace negative thoughts with a more realistic view that will build them up rather than tearing them down.

# Chapter 9: Dialectical Behavior Therapy

Dialectical Behavior Therapy is more like a positive form of psychotherapy that can be tailored to treat those with some form of borderline personality disorder.

More like a form of "talk therapy," DBT focuses on the psychosocial elements of treatment. Its theory is based on the premise that some people's behavior is so extreme that their reaction to romantic, familial, or social relationships is a manner that is far removed from the norm.

Those who fall into this category experience emotional extremes where their arousal levels can happen very quickly and their emotions are at such a peak that the reactions are at a very high level, taking them much longer to return to normal after an episode. They generally see things only in black or white with extreme emotional outbursts that can leave quite a bit of damage in their wake.

Because of this, they find themselves falling into one problem after another with no internal ability to manage their emotions. Therefore, they get no relief when their emotions spiral out of control. DBT is made up of three different elements:

**Support-Oriented:** Identifying their strengths and learning how to use them to help them feel better about themselves.

**Cognitive-Based:** Identifying the negative thought patterns and finding new ways to cope with triggering events so that their lives are more stable.

**Collaborative:** Rooting out underlying problems by working through assignments, active role-play, and learning self-soothing practices, so they can manage their own outbursts.

Through each of these sessions, the focus will be on two primary components:

1. **Structured Individual Psychotherapy Sessions**

Working with a therapist in a one-on-one session, patients will learn problem-solving behavior and openly discuss very specific issues that may have occurred in the past. These challenges could be anything from suicidal tendencies to self-mutilation. The more serious the issue, the more priority it should be given when working with the therapist. Minor issues may be assigned for the patient to deal with as homework.

During these sessions, you may also learn certain behaviors that can be applied to interrupt the negative habits. This adaptive behavior will have an emphasis on helping you to manage your emotions in the face of trauma much better. The objective here is to work towards a more socially acceptable behavior, so you can have better relationships with others.

## 2. Group Therapy Sessions

In group therapy, patients work their way through four different modules where they are taught practical skills they can rely on to help them cope with their negative patterns. Each skill has its own unique quality that can be used to minimize the negativity in their heads.

**Mindfulness:** A form of meditation where patients are helped to be more aware of their circumstances and the triggers that are causing their behaviors. Through mindfulness, they are taught how to observe, describe, and participate in their own thought processes as a neutral party. Then, with the use of special exercises, they learn how to recognize the triggers in their own mind, so they are better able to manage those reactions.

**Interpersonal Effectiveness:** Through practice sessions, they learn how to interact with others in a variety of scenarios. The process they go through is very similar to what is taught in many assertiveness training programs. Each session focuses on specific strategies to employ when getting to where they can ask for what they need, refuse things they don't, and specific coping mechanisms for when they are dealing with conflict.

**Distress Tolerance:** With distress tolerance, patients are given better ways to cope with disappointing and distressing circumstances. They learn how to accept things in a nonjudgmental manner. Rather than focusing on the negative, they will be better able to deal with real life situations that happen without their approval. Through this module, they are prepared with self-soothing techniques and other coping mechanisms that will reduce negative emotions and behavior.

**Emotional Regulation:** Learning how to regulate emotions is the key to managing negative behavior. Through the emotion regulation module, patients learn how to recognize the signs of oncoming intense emotions and use their coping strategies to manage them better. In this phase, they will be expected to address different emotional aspects including:

- Properly identifying and labeling their emotions when they arise.
- Recognizing the common obstacles that have been getting in the way of changing negative emotions.
- Lowering their susceptibility to negative emotions.
- Developing strategies to create more positive emotional experiences.
- Techniques that allow them to use their mindfulness to enhance positive emotions.
- They will also learn how to suppress their natural tendency long enough to choose another behavioral option opposite of what their instincts will do.
- They are given strategies they can utilize in distressful situations that will boost their tolerance levels.

With DBT, there are two main components, but because those that need CBT are most likely dealing with behavioral issues, they will focus most of their lessons in a group therapy environment, so they are able to practice their new skills and strategies they will need when interacting with others. DBT is still a relatively new program, but even so, it has already received recognition as a gold standard method of psychological treatment.

# PART IV

# Chapter 1: Self-Care Is the Best Care

*"It is so important to take time for yourself and find clarity. The most important relationship is the one you have with yourself."*

-Diane Von Furstenberg

Self-care is any activity that we deliberately do to improve our own well-being, whether it is physical, emotional, mental, or spiritual. The importance of taking care of one's self cannot be denied, as even health care training focuses on making sure healthcare workers are caring for themselves. If you do not take care of yourself, eventually, every other aspect o your life will fall apart, including your ability to help others.

This is a very simple concept, yet it is highly overlooked in the grand scheme of things. People lack the tendency to look after themselves and put their needs before anyone else. Good self-care is essential to improving our mood and reducing our anxiety levels. It will do wonders for reducing exhaustion and burnout, which is very common in our fast-paced world. It will also lead to positive improvements in our relationships.

One thing to note is that self-care does not mean forcing ourselves to do something we don't like, no matter how enjoyable it is to other people. For example, if your friends are forcing you to go to a party you rather not attend, then giving in is not taking care of yourself. If you would rather stay in and watch a movie, then that's what you should do, and it will be better for your well-being.

## How Does Self-Care Work

It is difficult to pinpoint exactly what self-care is, as it is personal for everybody. Some people love to pamper themselves by going to the spa, while others enjoy physical activities like hiking, biking, or swimming. Some individuals take up art or other hobbies, like writing or playing a musical instrument. These activities are all different but will have the same type of benefits for the individuals engaging in them.

The main factor to consider when engaging in self-care is to determine if you enjoy the activity in question. If not, then it's time to move on. Self-care is an active choice that you actually have to plan out. It is time you set aside for yourself to make sure all of your needs are met. If you use a planner of any sort, make sure to dedicate some space for your particular self-care activities. Also, let people who need to know about your plans so you can become more committed. Pay special attention to how you feel afterward. The objective of any self-care activity is to make yourself feel better. If this is not happening, then it's time to change the activity.

While self-care, as a whole, is individualized, there is a basic checklist to consider.

- Create a list of things you absolutely don't want to do during the self-care process. For instance, not checking emails, not answering the phone, avoiding activities you don't enjoy, or not going to specific gatherings, like a house party.

- Eat nutritious and healthy meals most of the time, while indulging once in a while.

- Get the proper amount of sleep according to your needs.

- Avoid too many negative things, like news or social media.

- Exercise regularly.

- Spend appropriate time with your loved ones. These are the people you genuinely enjoy and not forced relationships.

- Look for opportunities to enjoy yourself and laugh.

- Do at least one relaxing activity a day, like taking a bath, going for a walk, or cooking a meal.

Self-care is extremely important and should not be an anomaly in your life.

## How Does Self-Care Improve Self-Esteem and Self-Confidence?

To bring everything full circle, self-care plays a major role in improving self-esteem and self-confidence. It is easy to see how taking care of yourself will also make you feel better about yourself overall. All of these are actually inter-related, and a lack of one showcases a lack of the other. While caring for yourself also improves your self-esteem and self-confidence, not having self-esteem or self-confidence also leads to a lack of self-care. Basically, you believe that you are not good enough to be taken care of.

People with high self-esteem and self-confidence value themselves as much as they value others, and have no issues with making sure they're taken care of. They realize that it does not make them selfish or inconsiderate to think in this manner. Even if other people try to make them feel that way, a self-confident person will just brush off the criticism. An important thing to note is that when you take care of yourself, it does not mean you don't care about other people. It simply means you have enough self-love to not place yourself on the backburner.

Many people work so hard to try and please everyone else. This is one of the telltale signs of low self-esteem. While they're busy worried about other peoples' needs, their own get neglected, which will wear them down over time. The more they're unable to please someone, the harder they will try. What people in this situation don't realize is that some people are impossible to please, and it is not their responsibility to please them. That is up to the individual.

Poor self-care will eventually lead to poor self-image. It is possible that a person already has this initially. Self-care includes taking care of your hygienic and grooming needs. If you don't take the time to make yourself look good, this will significantly impact the value you place on yourself. When you are t work, among your friends, or just walking around town, not feeling like you look good will ultimately make you feel like you don't belong anywhere. Your confidence levels will plummet due to this.

Your health is another aspect to consider. Poor self-care means bad sleeping habits, unhealthy diets, lack of exercise, and more self-destructive behaviors. Your poor health practices can result in chronic illnesses down the line, like heart disease or diabetes. Once again, diminished health will lead to reduced self-confidence and self-esteem. Ask yourself now if putting other people ahead of you is worth it? I've got some news for you. The people who demand the most from you are probably looking out for themselves first.

The less a person takes care of themselves, the more their self-esteem and self-confidence will decline. It turns into a vicious downward cycle. This is why it is important to focus on all of these areas equally. When you find yourself neglecting your own self-care practices, it is time to shift your direction and bring your attention back to your needs. Ignoring your needs will ultimately lead to your fall. We will discuss specific practices and techniques for improving self-care in the next chapter.

# Chapter 2: What Does Good Self-Care Look Like?

## Good Self-Care Practices

The following are some ways that good self-care will look like. If you find yourself having these qualities, then you are on the right path.

### Taking Responsibility for Your Happiness

When you engage in self-care, it is truly self-care. This means you only rely on yourself, and nobody else, to make sure your needs are met. You realize that your happiness is no one else's responsibility but your own. You alone have the ability to control your outcomes. As a result of this independence, you will develop the skills and attitude you need to care for your own physical, mental, emotional, and spiritual well-being.

### You Become Assertive With Others

People often take assertiveness for rudeness. This is not true, but if people believe that standing firm for what you want is rude, then that's their problem. Once you reach a certain mindset where self-care is important to you, then you will be unapologetically assertive. This means you have the ability to say "no" with confidence and stand by it. "No" is a complete sentence, and people will realize that quickly when they hear it from you.

### You Treat Yourself As You Would a Close Friend

It's interesting how we believe that other people deserve better treatment from us than we do ourselves. We have a tendency to put our best friends in front of us, no matter how detrimental it is to our lives. This behavior stops once we engage in proper self-care. At this point, you will treat yourself as good as, or even better, than you treat your most beloved friends.

## You Are Not Afraid to Ask for What You Want

Once you learn to take care of yourself, you also see your value increase within your mind. This means having an understanding that your voice, opinion, and needs matter, just like anybody with high self-esteem and self-confidence, would. As a result, you will not be afraid to ask for what you want, even if you might not get it.

## Your Life Is Set Around Your Own Values

Once you practice self-care, you learn to check in with yourself before making important decisions. You always make sure the choices you are about to make line up with your purpose and values. If they go against them, then it's not a path you choose. This goes for the career you choose, where you decide to live, and the relationships you maintain in your life.


While all of the traits are focused on self, but it will lead to better relationships with other people too. When you practice self-care, you are in a better state in every aspect of your being. This gives you the ability to take care of and help those you need you, as well. Self-care is not an option, but a necessity, and it must never be ignored. Taking care of yourself is not selfish, no matter what anybody tells you. If someone tries to make you feel guilty over this matter, then consider distancing or removing them from your life. You are not obligated to maintain relationships with people.

# Chapter 3: Demanding Your Own Self-Care

We went over the importance of self-care, and now we will focus on making it a reality in your life. If you want self-care to occur, you must be willing to demand it. The world is full of people who expect you to be at there beck-and-call every moment of the day. Some of these individuals are those who are closest to us, like friends or family members. This can make it harder to make our demands heard, but there is no way around it. Taking care of yourself is not an idea you can budge on. It is extremely important. We will go over several ways to maintain your ability for self-care in your life and provide detailed action steps to help you progress in this area.

## Setting Healthy Boundaries

One of the biggest obstacles to self-care is other people who surround you. These are the true selfish individuals, whether they realize it or not, who believe they can barge in on your life and deserve all of your attention. They will take advantage of you, and if you are not careful, they will completely gain control of your emotions, and even your life. For proper self-care to occur, you must set firm and healthy boundaries with people. The following are steps that need to become mainstays in your life.

### Identify and Name Your Limits

You must understand what your emotional, physical, mental, and spiritual limits are. If you do not know, then you will never be able to set real boundaries with people. Determine what behaviors you can tolerate and accept, and then consider what makes you feel uncomfortable. Identifying and separating these traits will help us determine our lines.

## Stay Tuned Into Your Feelings

Two major emotions that are red flags that indicate a person is crossing a barrier are resentment or discomfort. Whenever you are having these feelings, it is important to determine why. Resentment generally comes from people taking advantage of us or feelings of being unappreciated. In this instance, we are likely pushing ourselves beyond our limits because we feel guilty. Guilt-trips is a weapon that many people use to get their way. It is important to recognize when someone is trying to make you feel guilty because they are way overstepping their boundaries. Resentment could also be due to someone imposing their own views or values onto us. When someone makes you feel uncomfortable, that is another indication of a boundary crossed. Stay in tune with both of these emotions.

## Don't Be Afraid of Being Direct

With some people, setting boundaries is easy because they have a similar communication style. They can simply read your cues and back off when needed. For other individuals, a more direct approach is needed. Some people just don't get the hint that they've crossed a line. You must communicate to them in a firm way that they have crossed your limits, and you need some space. A respectful person will honor your wishes without hesitation. If they don't, then that's on them. Your personal space is more important than their feelings.

## Give Yourself Permission to Set Boundaries

The potential downfalls to personal limits are fear, self-doubt, and guilt. We may fear the other person's response when we set strong boundaries. Also, we may feel guilty if they become emotional about it. We may even have self-doubt on whether we can maintain these limits in the long run. Many individuals have the mindset that in order to be a good daughter, son, parent, or friend, etc., we have to say "yes" all the time. They often wonder if they deserve to have boundaries and limits with those closest to them. The answer is, yes, you do. You need to give yourself permission to set limits with people because they are essential to maintaining healthy relationships too. Boundaries are also a sign of self-respect. Never feel bad for respecting yourself.

## Consider Your Past and Present

Determine what roles you have played throughout your life in the various relationships you have had. Were you the one who was always the caretaker? If so, then your natural tendency may be to put others before yourself. Also, think about your relationships now. Are you the one always taking care of things, or is it a reciprocal relationship? For example, are you always the one making plans, buying gifts, having dinner parties, and being responsible for all of the important aspects of the relationships? If this is the case, then tuning into your needs is especially important here. If you are okay with the dynamics of the relationship, then that's fine. I can't tell you how to feel. However, if you feel anger and resentment over this, then it's time to let your feeling be known, unapologetically.

## Be Assertive

Once again, this does not mean being rude, even though some people will interpret it that way. Being assertive simply means being firm, which is important when reminding someone about your boundaries. Creating boundaries alone is not enough. You also have to stand by them and let people know immediately if they've crossed them. Let the person know in a respectful but strong tone that you are uncomfortable with where they're going, and they need to give you some space. Assertive communication is a necessity.

## Start Small

Setting boundaries is a skill that takes a while to develop, especially if it's something you've never done before. Therefore, start with a small boundary, like no phone calls after a certain time at night. Make sure to follow through; otherwise, the boundary is worthless. From here, make larger boundaries based on your comfort level.

## Eliminating Toxicity and Not Caring About Losing Friends

If you plan on making self-care a priority in your life, I think that's great, and so should you. However, some people will have a problem with this. People don't always like it when their friends, family members, or acquaintances, etc., put themselves at the forefront of their lives. Once again, that is their problem, not yours. What is your problem, though, is distancing or even eliminating these individuals from your life. We will go over that in this section because part of self-care is eliminating toxicity from your life and not feeling bad about it.

### Don't Expect People to Change

While everyone deserves a chance to redeem themselves, there comes the point where we must accept that people cannot change by force. They have to find it within themselves to make this change, and it is not our responsibility to do so. You may yearn to be the one who changes them, but it's usually a hopeless project. Toxic individuals are motivated by their problems. They use them to get the attention they need. Stop being the one to give it to them.

### Establish and Maintain Boundaries

I already went in-depth on this, so I won't revisit it too much here. Just know that toxic people will push you to work harder and harder for them, while you completely ignore your own needs. This is exhausting and unacceptable. Create the boundaries you need with these individuals based on your own limits.

## Don't Keep Falling for Crisis Situations

Toxic people will make you feel like they need you always because they are constantly in a crisis situation of some sort. It is a neverending cycle. When a person is in a perpetual crisis, it is of their own doing. They often create drama purposely to get extra attention. You may feel guilty for ignoring them, but remember that their being manipulative and not totally genuine.

I am not saying that you can't ever help someone who is going through a hard time. Of course, you can. Just don't start believing that you're responsible for their success or failure.

## Focus on the Solution

Toxic individuals will give you a lot to be angry and sad about. If you focus on this, then you will just become miserable. You must focus on the solution, which, in this case, is removing drama and toxicity from your life. Recognize the fact that you will have less emotional stress once you remove this person from your life. If you let them, they will suck away all of your energy.

## Accept Your Own Difficulties and Weaknesses

A toxic person will know how to exploit your weaknesses and use them against you. For example, if you are easy to guilt-trip, they will have you feel guilty every time you pull away from them. If you get to know yourself better and recognize these weaknesses, then you can better manage them and protect yourself. This goes along with creating self-awareness, which we discussed in chapter two. When you accept your weaknesses, you can work on fixing them and balance them with your strengths.

## They Won't Go Easily

Recognize that a toxic individual may resist being removed from your life.

Actually, if they don't resist, I will be pleasantly surprised. They may throw tantrums, but this is because they can't control or manipulate you anymore. They will even increase their previous tactics with more intensity. It is a trap, and you must not fall for it. Stay firm in your desire to leave and keep pushing forward. If they suck you back in, good luck trying to get out again.

## Choose Your Battles Carefully

Fighting with a toxic person is exhausting and usually not worth it. You do not need to engage in every battle with them. They are just trying to instigate you.

## Surround Yourself With Healthy relationships

Once you have removed a toxic person, or persons, from your life, then avoid falling into the trap with someone else. Fill your circle with happy and healthy relationships, so there is no room for any toxicity. Always remember the signs of a toxic person, so you can avoid them wholeheartedly in the future.

## How to Focus on Self-Care

Now that we have worked to set boundaries and eliminate toxic people from our lives, it is time to focus on ourselves and the self-care we provide. The following are some self-care tips, according to psychologist, Dr. Tchiki Davis, Ph.D.

## Pay Attention to Your Sleep

Sleep is an essential part of taking care of yourself. You must make it part of your routine because it will play a huge role in your emotional and physical well-being. There are many things that can wreak havoc on your sleep patterns, like stress, poor diet, watching television, or looking at your phone as you're trying to fall asleep. Think about your night routine. Are you eating right before bed or taking in a lot of sugar and caffeine? Are you working nonstop right up until bedtime? Have you given yourself some time to wind down before going to sleep? All of these factors are important to consider, as they will affect your sleep patterns. If you can, put away any phones, tablets, and turn off the television at least 30 minutes before you plan on going to bed.

## Take Care of Your Gut

We often neglect our digestive tract, but it plays a major role in our health and overall well-being. When our gut is not working well, it makes us feel sluggish, bloated, and nonproductive. Pay attention to the food you eat as it will determine the health of your gut. It is best to avoid food with excess salt, sugar, cholesterol, or unhealthy fats. Stick to foods that are high in fiber, protein, healthy fats, and complex carbs. Some good options are whole grains, nuts, lean meats, fruits and vegetables, beans, and fish.

## Exercise and Physical Activity Is Essential

Regular exercise is great for both physical and mental health. The physical benefits are obvious. However, many people do not realize that exercise will help the body release certain hormones like endorphins and serotonin. These are often called feel-good hormones because they play a major role in affecting our mood in a positive way. The release of these hormones will give us energy too, which will make us want to exercise more. Once exercise becomes a habit, it will be hard to break. Decide for yourself what your exercise routine will be, whether it's going to the gym, walking around the neighborhood, or playing a game of tennis.

## Consider a Mediterranean Diet

While this is not a dietary book, the Mediterranean diet is considered the healthiest diet in the world because of its extreme health benefits. The food groups and ingredients that are used will increase energy, brain function, and has amazing benefits like heart and digestive tract health. The food also does not lack flavor, which shatters the myth that healthy food does not taste good.

## Take a Self-Care Trip

Even if you are not much of a traveler, getting away once in a while can do wonders for your mental health. So often, our environment will make us feel stressed out, and it's good to remove ourselves from it for a couple of days. You do not have to take a trip abroad here. Of course, that is certainly an option. A simple weekend trip is perfectly fine. Just get yourself out of your normal routine and be by yourself for a while.

## Get Outside

Nature and sunlight can be great medicines. It can help you reduce stress or worry, and has many great health benefits. Doing some physical activity outside, like hiking or gardening, are also great options.

## Bring a Pet Into Your Life

Pets can bring you a lot of joy, and the responsibility they come with can boost your self-confidence by having to care for another living creature. Dogs are especially great at helping to reduce stress and anxiety. Animal therapy has been used to help people suffering from disorders lie PTSD, as well.

## Get Yourself Organized

Organizing your life and doing some decluttering can do wonders for your mental and emotional health. Decide what area of your life needs to be organized. Do you need to clear your desk, clean out the fridge, or declutter your closet? Do you need to get a calendar or planner and schedule your life better? Whatever you can do to get yourself more organized, do it. Being organized allows you to know how to take better care of yourself.

## Cook Yourself Meals At Home

People often neglect the benefits of a good home-cooked meal. They opt, instead, for fast-food or microwave dinners. These types of meals will make you full but will lack in essential nutrients that your body needs. Cooking nutritious meals at home will allow you to use the correct ingredients, so you can feel full and satisfied. Cooking alone can also be great therapy for people.

## Read Regularly

Self-help books are a great read. However, do not limit yourself to these. You can also read books on subjects that you find fascinating or books that simply provide entertainment.

## Schedule Your Self-Care Time

Just like you would write down an appointment time in your planner, also block out specific times for self-care activities. Stick to this schedule religiously, unless a true emergency comes up. This means that if a friend calls you to go out, you should respectfully decline their request and focus on yourself.

# Chapter 4: How to Be Happy Being Alone

The final section of this book will focus on being alone and how to be happy about it. When you start engaging in self-care, you will also be spending much more time by yourself. A lot of people have a hard time dealing with this concept, especially if they're used to being around people all the time. However, for proper self-care, you have to be okay with being alone once in a while.

## Accept Some Alone Time

The following are some tips to help you become happy with being alone. Soon, you will realize that your own company is the best kind.

### Do Not Compare Yourself to Others

We are referring to your social life here. Do not compare to others, and do not feel like you must live as others do. If you do this, you may become jealous of a person's social circle or lifestyle. It is better to focus on yourself and what makes you happy. If you plan on spending significant time alone, then you cannot pay attention to what other people are doing.

### Step Away From Social Media

If strolling through your social media page makes you feel left out, then take a step back and put it away for a while. During self-care moments, you are the focus, not what is happening with others online. Also, what people post on their pages is not always true. Many individuals have been known to exaggerate, or even flat-out lie on social media platforms. You may be feeling jealous or left out for no reason. Try banning yourself from social media for 24-48 hours, and see how it makes you feel.

## Take a Break From Your Phone

Avoid making or receiving calls. Let the important people in your life know that you will be away from your phone for a while, so they don't worry. When you are alone, really try to be alone.

## Allow Time for Your Mind to Wander

If you feel unusual about doing nothing, it is probably because you have not allowed yourself to be in this position for a while. Carve out a small amount of time where you stay away from TV, music, the internet, and even books. Use this time to just sit quietly with your thoughts. Find a comfortable spot to sit or lie down, then just let your mind wander and see where it takes you. This may seem strange the first time, but with practice, you will get used to the new freedom.

## Take Yourself on a Date

You don't need to be with someone else to enjoy a night out on the town. Take a self-date and enjoy your own company for a while. Go to a movie by yourself, stop by a nice restaurant, or just go do an activity you enjoy. If you are not used to hanging out alone, give it some time and you will become more comfortable with it. Take yourself on that solo date.

## Exercise

We have mentioned exercise and physical activity a lot, but that's because it has so many great benefits related to self-care. Exercising will uplift your mood, and make it more enjoyable to be by yourself. Those feel-good hormones will provide a lot of benefits during these times.

## Take Advantage of the Perks of Being Alone

Some people have spent so much time with other people that they've forgotten the perks of being alone. There are many to consider. First of all, you do not have to ask anyone's permission to do anything; you will have more personal space, can enjoy the activities you want to do, and don't have to worry about upsetting anyone. If you want, you can even have a solo dance party in your living room, Tom Cruise style. There are many advantages to being alone, so use them.

## Find a Creative Outlet

It is beneficial to use some of your alone time to work on something creative. This can be painting, sculpting, music, writing, or any other creative endeavors. In fact, you can get out the watercolors and start fingerpainting. Creativity will bring a lot of joy into your life. It will make you happier about being alone.

## Take Time to Self-Reflect

Being alone will give you the opportunity to self-reflect on your life. You won't care so much about being alone when you are coming up with important answers to your life.

## Make Plans for Your Future

Planning out your life for five or ten years down the line will give you something important to do, and something to look forward to. Alone time is the perfect opportunity to determine these plans.

## Make Plans for Solo Outings

Plan your solo outings based on what you like to do, whether it's a farmer's market, hiking, riding your bike, or going camping alone. Mak plans that will excite you, and you will be taking care of yourself while also being okay alone.

There are numerous topics that we went over in this chapter, but they all relate back to one theme: Self-care. Always remember that to take proper care of yourself, you must consider the following ideas:

- Setting Boundaries
- Avoiding and ridding yourself of toxic people
- Focus on yourself and your needs
- Be okay with being alone

Focus on these areas, and you will be demanding your own self-care without ever apologizing for it.

CPSIA information can be obtained
at www.ICGtesting.com
Printed in the USA
LVHW052247011020
667643LV00002B/108